ST. MICHAEL PARISH LIBRARY

To Borrow books:

1. Write your name on the card that is in the pocket in the back of the book. + *Tel. #*

2. REMOVE card from the pocket and place it in FILE BOX marked "BOOKS OUT".

3. Suggested time of loan of books is 3 WEEKS.

4. When you return the book, place it in the box marked "BOOKS RETURNED".

5. DO NOT return book to shelf.

Thank you very much and happy reading

Who Will Teach Me?

A Handbook for Parents

by
Joseph F. Girzone

Richelieu Court, Publishers
Albany, New York

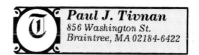

308.874
GIR
Acknowledgements

I am grateful to my family and friends who so kindly offered advice and suggestions during the preparation of this book. I am particularly grateful to my sister, Lorraine, and her husband Lester Bashant, for the totally dedicated assistance they have provided over these many months of difficult work. To repay them would be impossible.

My debt to my mother and father who molded my thinking and set me on the course of my life is inestimable.

To all these I happily dedicate this book.

PUBLISHED

BY

RICHELIEU COURT PUBLICATIONS, INC.
PO BOX 13264
ALBANY, NY 12212-3264

Library of Congress Catalogue Card Number 82-80555
ISBN 0-911519-69-6

836

PREFACE

Christianity is a way of life that should deeply affect the personality of everyone who commits his life to Christ. When a person becomes captivated by the beauty of Jesus' life and allows it to affect his own life, it insinuates itself into the very fabric of daily living. Every thought, every feeling, every attitude becomes colored by the intimacy of Jesus' friendship.

Because of the nature of this relationship, it is most effectively transmitted from one generation to another through the family itself. The atmosphere in the family, the delicate shades of feeling expressed by parents, the intimacy and complexity of the relationships between parents and children, provide the natural vehicle for passing on these rich and sensitive values to young people.

Churches have traditionally set up highly structured programs to teach children in a systematic way about the teachings of the church. These programs, as well-intentioned as they may be, can only provide support for the work parents should have already done with their children. They can in no way be a substitute for the vital role parents must play in the development of solid Christian values in their children.

However, there are some basic ideas which have an immense effect on the life of children and which, if they are not taught sensitively enough, can have tragic repercussions in later life. I share with you in the following pages a discussion about some of these ideas in the hope that it will provide help in the development of healthy Christian attitudes in our young people.

The life of Jesus is so beautiful that, when imitated, it can serve to bring out the best in human nature, and produce in the lives of those who follow it, a personality that transcends the merely human, and radiates a beauty, a joy and a freedom that reflects something of the divine in Jesus, and helps one to realize the value of the precious treasure which he shared with us in becoming human.

MOLDING ATTITUDES

One of the holiest persons I know once said to me, "I can't stand religion; it is too far removed from the life of the people." And that person is not alone in his thinking. Many good people have strange ideas about religion which are often fostered in the home by parents who are unaware of the effect their thinking has on the lives of their children.

I think it might be good for us to begin our discussion about religion by developing a precise idea of what we mean by religion. For the purpose of this book we do not intend to look upon religion as merely the worship of God. Nor do we intend to look upon religion as only the belief in the doctrines of a particular religion. What we mean by religion is a person's attitude toward God, and how that attitude affects all other attitudes, toward people, towards the person himself, toward events in life, toward all of creation. In short, what we mean by religion is the sum and total of a person's attitudes toward life.

Looked at from this point of view, we can see that everybody has a religion of some sort, a set of values by which he judges and evaluates every person and happening in his life, and determines how he will respond to other people and events. We can see that even though a person may say he is a

Catholic or a Presbyterian, or a member of a particular denomination, that is a very superficial description, because an individual's real religion involves a lot more than the doctrines of a particular sect. It is about religion at this much more profound and all-embracing level that we are concerned in this book.

To be more concrete, a child may be taught that God made him "to know Him, to love Him and to serve Him in this world, and to be happy with Him in the next." That's what his religion teaches him. But, by his parents' own attitudes, as manifested by the way they live their lives, the child may learn to believe that interest in self is the most important goal here on earth, and how he can use other people to attain that goal. That becomes the child's real religion.

With that viewpoint as the driving goal of his life, you can easily see how it will affect his behavior towards people, things and, particularly, money.

To take another example. A teacher may teach in religion class that Jesus died for us and he expects us to sacrifice for one another, and to share with others, and to be concerned about others. That kind of teaching becomes almost incomprehensible to a child whose father comes home bitter about people he's met during the day, and complaining that he's been cheated and victimized and made a fool of by this person or that person, and concluding that this is a "dog-eat-dog" world, and "you better get them before they they get you." Or if the child hears day after day, "Don't stick your neck out for anybody," "Take care of yourself, to hell with the other guy," or "Don't get involved, you'll always end up getting hurt," those slogans become the basis for the child's real religion, and no stranger in a religion class can possibly alter the almost constant brainwashing and indoctrination at home. The real motivating forces in a child's life, which become the child's real religion, are taught all day long in the home even though the parents may not realize they are teaching religion. For a stranger in a religion to teach a few religious ideas for a few minutes a week, borders almost on the ridiculous if he or she thinks they can give that child religion, or if the teacher feels he or she has an obligation to teach that child some kind of religion, since he doesn't get any at home.

I'll never forget one year I was teaching religion to the confirmation class. Every Wednesday afternoon the seventh and eighth graders were let out of school for release time classes. I used to stand out on the sidewalk to make sure there was no wild behavior as the small army came parading down the block. Every week there was one boy who walked by himself for fear of the others. But, they wouldn't leave him alone. They ridiculed and taunted him week after week. In the wintertime they pelted him with snowballs. I tried to protect the boy as well as I could, but it was futile. No matter how much I lectured the students in religion class about charity, the next week it would be just as bad. Obviously, my talking to them for a few minutes was nowhere near enough to offset the parents' indifference towards their children's insensitivity to the misery of others.

Of course, the most obvious example of the contradictory influence inflicted on children is on the part of parents who kick their kids off to church on Sunday morning and won't go themselves. The effect on those children is pathetic, and yet their parents think they are being responsible by sending their children to church. A final example is the teaching of respect for the name of God. What good is all the teaching by a stranger about respect due God's name if the child is exposed to a steady flow of blasphemy from his parents' lips, so the same language just automatically becomes normal part of the child's own vocabulary?

In spite of these shortcomings and other limitations of parents, it is still necessary for parents to assume the role of nurturing their own children in those areas that are vital to the development of character. And that really is religion. Parents may feel inadequate to the task, but they should not allow themselves to feel this way; their children need their guidance too much for it to be neglected.

We will try in this book to fill in for parents those areas where they may feel deficient, and offer some suggestions from our own experience over the years on how to develop healthy religious ideas and convictions in their children.

GOD

The most fundamental relationship for a child, after the parents' own relationship with their child, is the child's relationship with God. This is critical to a child's growth and will to a very great extent color many other relationships throughout his life. Because of this it is important that a child develop healthy and happy feelings about God. It is also important that the child not be taught to view God as reacting to us in too human a way. It is this mistake that gives rise to the many problems people have in relating to God, like the feeling that God is punishing me, or that God is constantly finding fault with my behavior, and is obsessed with human sin and failure, or that he is a highly critical being who is watching and waiting to fault us for every little thing. That idea of God does irreparable damage to our relationship with him, and undermines our peace of soul. It is essential that we have a happy feeling about God. When we think of him, it should bring us joy, and not dredge up guilt feelings.

It is this anthropomorphic or human concept of God that prompts us to see God as human like us and reacting to situations the way we would. So, when we do something wrong, we naturally feel that God is angry or sad or disappointed and will react by getting angry or punishing. That makes us frightened, especially knowing the tremendous power God has and the unlimited number of ways he can get even with us.

Fortunately, God is not that way. If he were there would have to be a reward and a punishment for every detail of our life. It is only human beings who feel they have to punish because they let their human feelings get in the way of their judgment. They become offended and have to get even. God would have to be totally paranoid to be that way.

This is one reason we have to be so careful in reading the scriptures, especially the Old Testament, because the authors of the various books shared the prevalent view of the time that the gods, even the true God, were vengeful gods. God had a very difficult time trying to convince the Israelites that he was a merciful and forgiving God, and it doesn't come through very clearly in the scriptures because it is confused by the many contradictions in the way the authors portray God's behavior. Sometimes he's angry and violent; sometimes he's kind and merciful and forgiving. The reader doesn't know what to believe or how to take God. So, he ends up being frightened by a God who is so changeable. And it is precisely feelings like these that make us feel very uncomfortable with religion, and deprive us of so much joy and richness that God wanted to bring into our lives.

This is why it is so important that parents have a healthy and beautiful view of God themselves, so they can transmit to their children a good feeling about God. If I were a parent, I would be very careful about allowing a stranger to enter into this area of my children's growth. It is too delicate and has too great far-reaching effects on the children's lives. The problem is that every teacher has his or her own views of God which they can't help but instill into the children's minds, and if those views are not healthy, the children can be seriously damaged.

A number of years ago, a pastor asked a class of children to tell him what they thought God was like. The wide variety of descriptions is interesting. One child said God was like her little puppy, cuddly, furry and warm. One boy said God was like his father, tall, strong, and with a deep, booming voice. Another said God reminded him of his grandfather, who loved him and was kind to him, but didn't punish him like his father did. Every one of those ideas of God, as different as they were, deeply affected the spiritual growth of those children and their attitude toward religion. This is why it is so important for parents to take time and use imagination in trying to form a realistic and inspiring understanding of God in the minds of their children.

But it shouldn't stop there. A child's mind is only a part of his inner life. A child's feelings must also become involved with God, and a child can be damaged if he is not taught to have warm and trusting feelings about God.

Now, how do we begin to teach a child about God, a person whom no one has ever seen? As we said before, it is the feeling about God that is important for a child. Children do not think in abstract concepts. They feel. They relate and associate familiar things with things that are not familiar. That's why those children the pastor asked to describe God, described him in terms with which they were familiar. So, when parents are trying to teach very young children about God, they should start by talking about things the children have nice feelings about, even if, in the beginning, it is very simple. You can gradually add to the ideas and, in time, build up a more involved understanding of God. But, it is also important that parents don't describe God as a human being. Once that image becomes a part of a child's thinking about God, it is almost impossible to erase it. And it is precisely that image which so rigidly fixes God in a mere human mold, and starts the process of viewing God as responding to our behavior in the same way any human being would respond.

But, where do you start? As soon as a child is able to hear and respond, perhaps as early as a year and a half old. This may seem young, but I say this from experience. There are two young children whose parents I know well. They let me help them teach their children religion from infancy. I used techniques I developed myself, and tried to instill a warm, personal relationship between these children and God. I started teaching them when they were only infants; one of them, even before he could talk. Now one is thirteen, and the other is seven. The results have been most rewarding.

An important time to impress children is when you put them in the crib at night. Take time to talk to them. Even though they can't talk, they can hear and they can think, and they can imagine and have feelings about people. Their ability to understand the meaning of words comes a lot earlier than their ability to speak. So, you can have conversations with them that go far in developing thoughts and feelings, and providing nourishing material for their very active imaginations. For example, if a mother or father were to sit down near the crib and, after tucking the baby in and giving it its bottle. were to pray out loud so the baby could hear, the baby would sense that the mother or father was talking to someone that they could not see, someone very important. The child could hear the parents thanking God for giving them Peter or Mary or whatever the baby's name. In that simple prayer the child senses, in some way, that he came from God, and that his mother and father love God and have nice feelings for God. As this is repeated, it becomes a part of the child's thinking. Parents can also thank God for the sun and the moon, and the pretty snow and the rain, and the beautiful flowers. Of course, this must be done very simply. You can overdo it, and then defeat the purpose. Children are still very simple, and they can only grasp so much. But the basic feeling about God can be transmitted very effectively to a child in this way.

Another very effective way of teaching a child about God, is to take him for a walk, and show him flowers and other fascinating things, and tell him that God made those flowers, and made them pretty, so we would like them and they would make us happy. The same can be done when pointing out the sun and the beautiful blue sky, and the birds, and so many things in nature that fascinate babies. This is an important part of a child's education about God, because it makes the child realize, at a very early age, that God is very much a part of his family's life. And even though that may be about all you can teach a child at that age, the thought of God begins to develop deep roots and provides a solid basis for later development.

JESUS

Once a child is old enough to look at pictures in a book, you can have all kinds of fun teaching about Jesus' life. Children become fascinated with Bible stories. I used to visit the family with the children I taught religion to, perhaps, only once a week. But, as soon as I would walk in the front door, the baby, who was about two years old, would immediately get his Bible story book, and grab my arm and say, "Johnny Battis, Johnny Battis," which meant that he wanted me to read him the story about John the Baptist. But, rather than read the story, I would just explain the pictures. He would turn the pages to his favorite stories, and I would have to re-tell them. He loved the story about Jesus and the "debbil", and Jesus raising the dead girl to life. I don't know how many times I told the story about Jesus walking on the water, and Jesus raising Lazarus from the dead. When it came to the arrest of Jesus and the crucifixion, the reaction was touching. He would ask, "Jesus was so good, why did they hurt him?" And he would just sit and look at the picture of the crucifixion for the longest time.

But, there are problems in teaching about Jesus. You are faced with the very human Son of God, so the child sees God as a human being for the first time. You explain that Jesus is God's Son, and let it go at that for the time being.

That naturally raises questions in the child's mind, but they can be resolved later on, when he or she is able to understand a little more clearly. The story about the Holy Spirit hovering over Jesus, when John baptized him, is another problem that sticks in a child's mind and has to eventually be resolved.

I was delighted not too long ago by a conversation with Peter, who is now seven, when I was tucking him in one night.

He said, "I finally figured out about God." I asked him what he figured out and he said, "You know, about the three of them, God, and Jesus and the other guy." "You mean the Holy Spirit."

"Yeah." "Well, what did you figure out?" "That they're all really one. God is God, Jesus is God, and the other one is God; and when you know Jesus, you know the other two, what they're like, because they're all just like each other." Now, that was quite a deduction, and reminded me of the words of Jesus to Philip, when Philip asked Jesus to show him the Father. Jesus said, "Philip, when you see me you see the Father." So, you can see that that little boy was thinking about the problem for a long time until he finally resolved it for himself.

I hope I don't give the impression that this boy or his brother are hooked on religion. They aren't, but they have developed a curiosity about Jesus' life, more than about what the church teaches, and that is much more healthy. That close, warm relationship with Jesus nobody can take from them. It is now an indelible and deeply-rooted part of their life. And they enjoy it and feel very comfortable with God. Even as a teenager, the older one still likes his religion. He doesn't look at it as something he has to get away from because he's now growing up. If he had been taught religion as a set of rules and regulations and doctrines, which is negative, restrictive and depressive, then, as an adolescent, he would feel the inevitable need to assert his freedom from these repressive aspects of his childhood as so many teenagers do. But, having grown up with a beautiful and warm friendship with Jesus which in no way threatens his freedom or need for independence, he feels no need to rebel against religion. It is too beautiful a part of his life. And that is the way religion should be taught. Jesus didn't give us a church primarily, or a set of hard fast doctrines, but a way of life which he entrusted to the church. Jesus gave us his friendship and the assurance of his Father's love and care for us. He never taught doctrine or ethics. He taught us to love God and to care for one another. He taught us that we would one day live with him in his Father's house, if we were willing to accept his love and friendship and the life he offered us. It is theologians and so-called religious people, who have taken the beauty out of Jesus' life and reduced it to dogmas and morals, and legalistic concepts, and passed them off as "the teachings of the church." This has done irreparable damage to our relationship with God. It shifts our loyalties to a church or a hierarchy, rather than to the person of Christ. That confusion of loyalties complicates our whole practice of religion and makes it almost impossible for the average Christian to find the living Christ and the beautiful attitudes he offered us as our real religion. Without intending it, we, as religious leaders, have done the same thing to Jesus' religion that he condemned the scribes and pharisees for doing to Judaism. We have taken the love of God and his creation, and love of neighbor, and Jesus' sharing a new life and a new freedom, and reduced it to frozen theological formulas and quasi-magical rites, so that people can conclude that by observing the rites, like baptism, they can be Methodists, Catholics, Presbyterians or whatever, without ever making a commitment of their life to Christ. We have all but killed healthy religious feelings in people by our artificial and legalistic approach to religion. It is as if those who are teaching religion have never known the real, warm, flesh-and-blood Jesus, but just picked up books about his teachings and formulated a systematic classroom subject called religion. We are trying lately to break away from that, but the attempts are feeble because we are substituting concepts for the real Jesus. We have to teach the real Jesus, and everything else as merely an expression of his attitudes and his vision of reality. Rather than teaching sacraments as liturgical rites, we should be teaching sacraments as phases of growth in our life with Jesus. That serves to make the sacraments spontaneous and natural events in the story of our personal friendship or love affair with Jesus and would determine the way in which we would use the sacraments. It is much more beautiful for a person to come to the priest's or minister's house, and spontaneously pour out his heart over the failures of his life, while the clergyman consoles and strengthens him, and brings him back to Jesus, than to set up a table and a bible and two chairs in a confessional room in a church building and schedule people to come for forgiveness or absolution or reconciliation at specified times. The Holy Spirit doesn't work on our schedules. It is artificial and just a religious rite. If Jesus were here today, which way would he do it? Would we have to go and meet him in church? I think reconciliation is one sacrament that is better administered outside of church, though ritual reconciliation in church will always have its place and a certain value.

Teaching children to develop a personal closeness to Jesus is not as difficult as parents may think. And they should not be afraid of it. There is no reason why they can't take the gospels and, as the children are growing older, talk to them about the beautiful ideas Jesus taught; about God wanting us to look upon him as a kind and caring Father, about heaven, the beautiful place where God lives, and where he wants us to come and live with him when our life on earth is finished. It is inspiring for a child to see the unselfish goodness in the life of Jesus, and the care that he shows for even the simplest and the poorest people, and never asks anything from them but that they love God and care for one another. If children are taught to see Jesus as a person who really enjoyed life, and was free and happy and not preoccupied with sin and guilt, and wants us to have the same freedom, it can do wonders to the way they will feel about religion.

ATTITUDES TOWARDS SELF

Image of self is an all important attitude that parents must carefully develop in their children, starting at a very early age. From my own experience with children, I have observed that some children seem to be very sure of themselves, even as infants. Others seem to be timid and insecure, in spite of parents doing things that would foster feelings of security.

Some seem to have an innate aggressiveness. These basic attitudes have a strong effect on a child's behavior, and also on how he will view himself in his relationship with God later on. A timid child may grow up feeling very comfortable with a religion that is rigid and directs his life for him, but might view God as strongly judgmental and critical of human behavior, which conditions him to be highly critical of himself and makes him frightened of God.

On the other hand, a highly self-confident child could conceivably grow up having a carefree attitude towards God, feeling that God's O.K. and I'm O.K., but resenting a church or religious leaders who might try to direct his thinking or tell him how to live his life. So, attitudes about ourselves are a very important part of religious orientation, and parents should be keenly concerned about making fine adjustments in their children's attitudes towards themselves and how they feel about God. If a child is timid, that child should be taught not to be afraid of God, but to have a trust in God who is very caring and understanding, particularly when we make mistakes and do things out of weakness. If a child is inclined to be cocky or overly self-confident, he should be taught that God expects us to use our gifts and talents for him and that our lives must be productive of good, if we expect God to look favorably on us. We can't take our own goodness for granted, as if God is perfectly pleased with us just the way we are. Children who are strongly self-reliant should be taught that others have abilities and insights that they don't have, and they should always be willing to listen to others, even if they don't agree, and try to understand others' points of view. This will help the child to adjust, later on, when confronted with a pastor who might be authoritarian or opinionated, or with his church which might appear to dominate his life.

Many attitudes which children develop do not spring from their personalities, but are the result of parents' own expressed feelings. Children instinctively want to grow up. They feel the best way to do this is by imitating parents.

Parents should be sensitive to the effect their words and example have on their children and should be willing to take pains to help their children develop healthy feelings about others. Again, if a child is inclined to be self-confident, it may be difficult for that child to appreciate other children. He or she may tend to look down on other children, or be bossy or impatient. So, that kind of a child must be taught to respect the opinions of others, and treat others with respect, and not always insist on doing things his own way. It is also important to help children who are this way to notice and appreciate the abilities and talents of others. Granted, all of this takes time. But, that is what makes the raising of children such a beautiful and challenging career, realizing the wonderful complexity and potential that lies there in the children, waiting to be analyzed, and unraveled, and developed.

This developing of a child's awareness of himself may not seem to be a religious concept, but it is the basis of the child's relationships with other persons, and how a child relates to other people is very much a part of his religion.

SIN

Sin is a horrible word, with all the memories and feelings it evokes in so many of us. Webster defines sin as "the willful breaking of religious or moral law." Sin is so intimately tied up with law, that I don't think it is even healthy to mention the word to children. I know this will cause many to raise their eyebrows, and ask how do I expect parents to teach children the difference between right and wrong, if they can't tell the child that something is a sin.

But, we can teach right from wrong in different ways. The way it was done in the past produced a lot of unnecessary guilt, which did untold damage to many young people growing up. There is nothing that can turn a child away from religion more effectively than by convincing a child that he is always sinning, or that many things that he or she does are a sin. It makes a child only too conscious that there is a lot of evil in him. That produces the kind of guilt which tears us apart, and makes us feel that there is something seriously flawed in our personality. That is the basis for a great deal of sickness, both mental and physical, in many grown-ups.

We have to teach right from wrong in a way that is healthy, a way that will encourage young people to be good and still preserve a good image of themselves. How we go about this is critical. Again, what I write here is from my own practical experience in working with little children. I have found that, if a parent is always in a rush, the tendency is to take short-cuts in correcting children's behavior. It's a lot easier to tell a child, "Don't do that, that's a sin," as if just telling a child, automatically affects behavior. Teaching right from wrong has to be a well-thought-out process, and should be integrated into the child's friendship with Jesus. So parents might consider that children not be taught about sin, until they have been taught about Jesus, and have begun to express good feelings about Jesus. Once they do this, you can then begin to relate their own behavior to Jesus. For example, you have already taught the child how kind Jesus is. So, when you see the child doing something mean or unkind, you take the child aside and remind him of Jesus and of his friendship with Jesus, and tell him that, if he is a friend of Jesus, he will want to be like Jesus, and will be kind to people. It works, believe me! And it doesn't give the child a bad feeling of having broken a commandment that is punishable by God's justice. One day, one of the little boys I had been working with, had come home from school. He was very happy about something. When his mother asked him why he was so happy, he said there was a retarded girl in his class, whom nobody would play with. He remembered that Jesus was kind to everyone, even people whom nobody else liked, so he went over and played with the girl, and it made her so happy. That's the kind of positive behavior that parents should foster in their children. It's healthy and cultivates good feelings. A child can feel comfortable with that kind of religion.

SEX

Sex is a major pre-occupation today, even among children who are not yet adolescents. They see so much of it on television, they become very aware of it long before their emotional and psychological needs begin to stimulate an interest in the opposite sex. One of the flaws in the sex education programs is the lack of realization that it is not information the children need, (they know more about sex today at thirteen than most high school graduates knew a generation ago), but a strong conviction about the value of sex, and an understanding of the sacredness and beauty of relationships with persons of the opposite sex. It is because of a lack of appreciation of this that young people see nothing terribly wrong with using others to satisfy their own needs. And that, precisely, is the great tragedy of our culture's sick attitude towards sex. It has become the popular game that people play for personal fun, without seriously intending to make a personal commitment of themselves to each other. That, in turn, tends to cheapen and undermine even our ability to make a lifetime commitment to someone whom we genuinely admire. Using people has become a habit too deeply ingrained for us to change radically just because we have finally found the one person whose love we treasure.

Teaching our children about sex has to start at a very early age; not about the physical aspects of sex, but about respect for others, particularly, for persons of the opposite sex. There are differences between the sexes, even though many try to make believe there aren't. And those differences are more than just biological. Biological alone means both physical and chemical, and where chemistry is involved, the emotional and psychological are also involved. What the pure primitive female or male would be like, first coming from the hand of God, I don't think we'll ever be able to tell, but to demand that both are the same except for reproductive organs is frightfully dangerous. If a person is taught to believe that, it can destroy the person's ability to develop a healthy sexual identity, and ease a person into homosexual fantasies.

Since sex is the area of so much misery and agony in our society, it is essential that parents take the greatest pains to develop healthy feelings and attitudes in their children, if they want to guide them into a healthy adulthood.

How should parents go about this? First of all, there has to be a good relationship between a mother and father. I realize not many approach the ideal, and, in many cases, there is only one parent, so adjustments must be made. A child's feelings about his father and his mother help to develop the child's own sexuality. Many boys who have never been successful in developing good relationships with their fathers, and who have never been able to please them, still feel the need to attain the goal of being acceptable to a male figure, and feel drawn to male companionship as adolescents. So, it is critical that fathers play a role in the development of their children and not leave that work to the mother. The same is true for mothers and daughters. Another important factor to be aware of in molding a child's feelings about sex, is helping the child realize who he or she really is. Sometimes a mother may have wished she had a daughter instead of a son and frequently will treat the little boy as a girl for years, before she decides she has to finally treat him as a boy. That kind of upbringing can do irreparable damage to a child, and he may never be able to think as a boy should think or feel as a boy should feel, because, in his early years, he was taught daily to think of himself as a girl.

All of these things are a part of a child's religion, if we look at religion as our attitudes towards God, towards ourselves, and towards others. How we see ourselves in those relationships, goes a long way in forming our attitudes towards life. How a person feels about himself dramatically affects that person's religion.

Besides having a healthy relationship with a child, the parents must also form ideas and values in a child's mind, so that the child's subconscious feelings and attitudes about persons of the opposite sex are realistic and healthy. Our external behavior is determined greatly by our subconscious values. When boys and girls are growing up they rarely pay much attention to each other. Once a boy wakes up to sex, he will automatically want to experiment. And what is there to prevent him from giving in to those powerful urges he is experiencing for the first time? He has to have unusually powerful motives to restrain himself, and this is what is lacking in the training of children: the motivation which will help them to control their behavior when they are on their own. The trend in society today is to accept adolescent sexual activity and make it easier by freely teaching how to avoid the consequences and justifying whatever steps are taken to avoid problems, even to the extent of justifying abortion. That is a very unhealthy way to instill or maintain high standards of character in our young people.

How can parents instill in their children the ideals and motivation they need? Motivation comes from attitudes and values, and deep-seated convictions. If a mother and father impressed on their child's mind the sacredness of the human person no matter what the sex, and that our love of God should prompt us to respect each person, and if that idea was talked about frequently, it would become deeply embedded in a child's convictions. If a child was taught that the human body is the temple of God's presence and is sacred, that would become a part of the child's attitude toward others. If a child was also taught constantly not to use people for his own purposes, but to be sincere in his relationships with others, persons of the opposite sex included, that would become part of the motivational structure of a child's behavior pattern. If, besides all this, the child was taught that girls are special, and have a very special purpose in God's plan, which is sacred, and that God's unique power to create is intimately involved in the relationship between a man and a woman, that would be programmed into the subconscious feelings of the child. If all these attitudes were reinforced by a child's strong sense of his own dignity, and awareness of his deep friendship with Jesus, he would have powerful motives to help counteract the strong sexual drives of adolescence. But, strip him of all these convictions and how can he possibly be expected to control himself. And that is what is lacking in so many young people today. No amount of sex education will compensate. The most it will do is make young people efficient and expert players of the game, and help erode their already shabby attitudes towards persons of the opposite sex.

We might also add that a father and mother's own relationship with each other, and the respect they show towards one another, will teach the child how he should treat persons of the opposite sex. If a boy sees his father abusing and mishandling his mother, he most probably will end up treating women the same way. If a girl sees her mother demeaning her father and belittling him, she will find it very difficult not to humiliate men as ordinary way of acting towards men.

Sexual behavior is closely tied to self-image, as well as our attitudes towards others, and parents should use great care to foster healthy attitudes, if they expect normal sexual growth.

PLAY

I never thought I would have to emphasize play as part of our religious value system. But, lately, so many parents are driving their children to achieve, that I feel it is important for parents to understand the value of playing, and just enjoying pleasurable things in life, and teaching this value to their children. I realize that children don't have to be taught the value of play; love of play is quite natural to them. But, often parents drive their children to be doing things productive, and badger and ridicule them for wasting time, when they are just enjoying wholesome play. The children may not appear to be affected by it, and may continue to play as they always have, but they begin to develop guilty feelings when they are just relaxing, and not doing something positively productive. As they grow older, they will find it difficult to just relax, and enjoy the simple pleasures of life without feeling guilty.

Play and relaxation and the enjoyment of the pleasures found in God's creation is the natural tranquilizer God has given us. It replenishes our energies, it re-creates our spirits, it re-focuses our vision and helps to keep us balanced in our judgment; it deepens our awareness of the presence of God in creation and in our personal lives, it lifts up our spirits from depression, and helps us to bring joy into our own lives and the lives of others. For all of these reasons, children should be taught the value of play, and of setting time in their schedule for play and relaxation.

But, play is not just fun for children. Though parents may not realize it, play is really serious business for children, and they take it seriously. They don't realize it themselves, but it is an integral part of their learning process. For that reason, parents should take their children's play seriously, and should not look upon it as mere play with little or no value.

Children are never just playing. It may look like they are just playing a game or playing house, or being a bulldozer operator, or a policeman, or building skyscrapers. But, they are very serious about it, and they are learning and absorbing all kinds of information about things they are playing with, and about the mistakes they are making, and about what can be done and cannot be done with things. And if a child is playing with another child, he is also learning to develop socially. What seems to be play is very far from being just play.

Children become just as engrossed in their play as grow-ups do in their activities, and just like we wouldn't think of interrupting a grown-up who is in the middle of something exciting, so we should have some respect for children's feelings. Parents constantly frustrate them by making them stop doing something they are right in the middle of. We don't like to be stopped when we are in the middle of something enjoyable. It makes us angry. Children get angry too, but they are expected to keep it inside.

Our attitude towards what children are doing goes far in molding a child's image of himself and in developing a healthy sense of self-importance. A child takes his play seriously and during play sees himself in all kinds of important roles. When a parent becomes aggravated about something and off-handedly yells at a child deeply engrossed in, say, building a skyscraper or designing a car or building a highway in the dirt, and tells the kid to "get that damn junk the hell out of the way," it deflates and demeans a child, and helps to develop the attitude in a child that what he is doing is not really important. What parents have to realize is that what a child is doing is very important to him, and parents' attitude towards their child's interests helps to form the child's good or bad feeling about himself. Even children deserve respect; it is a lot easier for them to respect those who are kind to them, than it is to show respect to a person who frequently humbles or embarrasses them.

Perhaps the way to handle children's play, is to schedule the play time, and let the child play undisturbed during that time, knowing that, when the time is up, he or she is expected to pick things up and do whatever other chores that are scheduled.

Play is important for all of us, not just because of its natural tranquilizing effect on us, but because it also is an essential component of a normal healthy way of living. Children should be taught this, and also how to incorporate play into their lives in a way that's beautiful.

PERSONAL POSSESSIONS

Children develop a sense of ownership at a very early age. The instinct is innate. Little colored rattles and hanging things in a crib appeal to an infant, and it grabs hold of them and doesn't want to let go. As a child gets older, it wants everything it sees and becomes almost violent when someone tries to take things away. The need to possess is deeply rooted in our nature and should be dealt with by parents when the children are at a very young age.

Again, as Christians, we have a definite attitude that Jesus gave us about ownership and possessing things, and a healthy Christian mentality should be formed in the child. Fortunately, children love to please and frequently they try to please by giving things to others. This is often not easy, but their desire to please and get a response is greater at that moment than their attachment to what they are giving away. When parents notice this, they should take advantage of the situation and teach the child to share, by making a big fuss when the child offers something. This serves to encourage the child to enjoy giving and to break the fierce hold that the desire to possess has over the child.

I have found in my own experience that there are basically two types of people: those who are takers and those who are givers. Takers never seem to learn how to love or to give of themselves. Givers find real happiness in sharing and in giving of themselves. These basic attitudes affect almost every aspect of life and shape all our human relationships. So, it is important that parents consciously try to mold a healthy, well-balanced attitude towards possessing and sharing.

My own experience with the family I have been friends with, particularly the little ones, provided me with a wealth of insights into this area. I would like to share them with you.

When Peter was a little boy he was very possessive, perhaps, even more so than many children. He would take and hide in ingenious places all kinds of things he found appealing. He had a particular fondness for coins he collected from various sources; a whole jarful of quarters, dimes and nickels. Pennies, he never cared for. We all noticed the developing trait, so I suggested we try to encourage him to be more giving. At the time he was, I think, three years old. We all made a concerted effort to praise him profusely whenever he shared something. He liked that, and began to go out of his way to give. When people came to the house, he would always make it a point to give them something, like an orange or a banana. When I would leave, he would have a little bag of something for me to take home. A few days before Christmas, he called me up and asked if I would come over and take him shopping. When I arrived, he went upstairs, got his jar of money, and asked me to help him count it. We counted seventy-two dollars. Of course, this was done very secretively. He didn't want anyone in the the family to know what he was up to, though I managed to make his mother and father aware. He then told me he wanted to go shopping and buy presents for everyone in the family. Knowing how attached he was to that money, I could understand what it cost him to spend it on presents. But, he insisted on picking out each one himself, and wondered if what he picked would make that person happy. It was beautiful. I wouldn't let him spend all the money, but he did spend a good part of it. The joy on his face Christmas day, when each one got their present,was a thrill to experience. To this day he is still a shrewd little kid, but very giving.

His brother Joey never had a thing with money so he was always broke. But, around Christmas time, Joey would come up to my rectory, and spend hours making things in the ceramic class or painting pictures so he could have something he himself made for each one in the family. He was only nine then, so he had to put a lot of himself into those little presents.

I realize many parents won't feel comfortable with their children giving things away so freely, but this whole idea of giving has to be thoroughly thought out in terms of what attitude a Christian should have towards material possessions, and towards being giving persons. Parents naturally want to see their children taking care of themselves, and being shrewd in the way they handle their affairs, and they become concerned when they see their children being indifferent towards material things or being "too generous" to other people. They should be thinking of themselves and their families.

But, this idea of giving is tied in with a person's whole attitude towards human relationships. Children who are never taught to give seem never to learn to love, and they make miserable husbands or wives. So many of the problems married persons have brought to me over the years involved a person who was very giving married to a person who was unable to give. And it is not just material things that we are talking about; it is the ability to love and to give of one's self, to share time and feelings and one's experiences. Inability to share money and material things is a manifestation of the unhealthy kind of self-centeredness that destroys a person's ability to grow spiritually and as a human being. Giving persons are always beautiful people. Cheap people are always the butt of jokes and ridicule behind their backs, the kind of people we all try to discreetly avoid, because they don't know how to be friends; they use everyone, and it's just a matter of time before it's your turn.

So, when parents think about teaching their children to save, to be thrifty, and not too giving, they should be very aware of what kind of course they are setting for their children. It's not just a matter of saving, it's a whole philosophy of life they are teaching their children. And, ultimately, it's the parents themselves who will be most deeply hurt, because it is not the thrifty, miserly children who will be available when the parents need help in their old age, but the giving children who will take care of them. The others may do it, but for a price, or after they have made sure they will be well compensated in the parents' will. And that hurts deeply, but it is often the way parents have brought up the children, and they have learned their lessons only too well.

PRAYER

Most people hate to pray. Why? Prayer should be an enjoyable experience. If it is not, it's only because we have not learned how to pray. Prayer should be an outpouring of the emotions. This comes spontaneously when we feel strongly about something. Prayer merely directs those feelings to God as we include him in the expression of our experiences. Prayer is a catharsis and like any catharsis should give a sense of relief as we pour out our feelings. I can understand how a person would feel who had been taught to pray by merely saying memorized prayers, or reading prayers. Some may be able to put their feelings in gear with another's words, but ordinarily this kind of prayer can be stripped of one's own personal emotions, and unexpressive of what the person really feels. The prayer then becomes boring and a drudge. If we are forced to pray this way, we can learn to hate prayer.

Prayer should flow naturally and spontaneously from the soul. If we are convinced God is real and cares for us, it is only normal for us to want to share with him our feelings and experiences, good and bad, as we would with a friend. That's all that prayer is.

How should parents teach their children to pray? First of all, it should be natural and simple. When a child learns to talk, the parents should take turns talking to God, or to Jesus, with the child. If a parent senses something important happened to the child during the day which made a deep impression on the child, that could be the subject of a simple prayer or sharing with God that night, though prayer need not be limited only to bedtime. It can be spontaneous at odd times during the day. Helping a child share his experiences with God puts the child in touch with God and brings God in a very practical way into the child's life. Everything in life becomes an experience to be shared.

When a parent is talking to God with the child, the parent can gently and skillfully talk about the child's behavior during the day, and in a friendly and uncritical way, about other things the child did which were not too nice, and conclude by saying, for example, "Since you're my friend, God, I'm going to be better tomorrow." In this way you are pointing out to the child things he did wrong, but relating it to the child's friendship with God. You are not relating it to laws which have been violated and for which the child could be one day punished, and you are not awakening unhealthy feelings of guilt, but you are developing an awareness that what the child does is an expression of his friendship with Jesus. As the child's relationship with Jesus deepens, the effect on the child's behavior will also deepen.

To give another example of how this works. One day Joey was going to receive Communion. Before Communion he was telling Jesus he had taken his brother Rick's baseball and played with it. When he finished, he saw all the players' signatures were rubbed off. He told Jesus how badly he felt about it, and said he would tell his brother what he had done and apologize. Later in the day he did just that, as difficult as it was for him. Joey was eleven and Rick was eighteen. That kind of behavior and response was healthy and normal, and can provide the foundation for strong character development. There was none of the sick kind of guilty feelings that could have just as easily been his response to having taken something that didn't belong to him and destroyed its value.

Another important part of prayer is in developing a realization that God and the child have a real working partnership. God is not just some vague being who never answers when we talk to him, or the object of a one-way conversation. He is a friend who cares. Jesus is, by his own choice, our brother. He is the one who chose to strike up a friendship with us and wants to be our friend, with all that friendship entails. So, when you teach a child to pray, it is important to teach him to discuss problems with Jesus, to share with him things that are disturbing or frightening, and to ask for his advice or guidance.

However, it should be impressed on the child that God is not going to give him a direct response that can be heard. God is not restricted in the way he can communicate with us. He works quietly and subtly in our souls, by helping us to see things in a different light, or by suggesting new approaches or solutions to problems we may be facing. By teaching a child to listen to God, you are at the same time teaching the child to be thoughtful in difficult situations in life. In doing this you are teaching him not to panic in crises, but, in the context of communing with God, to ponder the problem and consider the range of options. This may not seem like much in the beginning, but it accomplishes wonders in training a child to approach serious problems with courage and patiently work them out. And that's an ability that is frightfully lacking in many adults.

In teaching a child to pray, a parent shouldn't emphasize asking God for things. That kind of prayer can lead to confusing and frustrating experiences. A child should be taught to trust God and realize that God knows what he needs, and will eventually grant what is genuinely needed. To pray for all kinds of specific things is meaningless. It can turn God into a genie whose function it is to grant wishes. The child should be taught that we are the creatures who should be concerned about what God wants of us. This doesn't mean that a child shouldn't be taught to ask for God's help in time of sickness or great need, but even that prayer should be expressed with a humble resignation to God's will.

If a child is taught to pray properly, it can be one of the most rewarding and beautiful facets of his life, and something that the child will treasure throughout his whole life, particularly when trying to decide on a vocation. If a young person has always been close to God, he will realize that God made us for a purpose and gave us all we need to do a special work for him. Rather than tell God what he is going to be, the young person will recognize the need to ask for God's guidance and direction in the work God has planned for him.

The important attitude in praying is the realization that our life is a partnership with God, and that he is vitally interested in us, and will guide and counsel and help us every step of the way. This presupposes a childlike trust in God and deepens our awareness of his place in every facet of our life. Parents should not be afraid to teach their children that kind of trust. It will not leave them vulnerable, but will expand their vision into dimensions they would never dream of if they were to walk alone through life.

RESPECT FOR OTHERS

Jesus, even though he was the Son of God, showed an exquisite respect for his fellow humans. We see it in the delicacy of his treatment of the widowed woman of Naim, who was burying her only son. We see it in the kindly way he treated Peter's mother-in-law. We see it in the courtesy with which he treated the Roman official, who wanted his servant cured. There are numerous other examples. Respect for the dignity of others was very much a part of the spirituality Jesus bequeathed to us, and it should be instilled in children when they are young. The way we treat others flows quite naturally from the attitude we have towards ourselves. To a great extent, this orientation is developed by the type of relationship parents develop with their children. Many parents like to be on intimate and very familiar terms with their children. They allow the children to relate to them on a personal and casual basis. They are reluctant to discipline them or be harsh in any way, feeling that they should discuss and reason with the children.

I have seen the effects of this in families over a twenty year period, and watching the results in adolescence was quite a shock. Parents who are too familiar with children and allow them to treat them as friends and not parents, erase the barriers that exist between parent and child. It may seem beautiful when the children are young, but as they grow older they begin to treat the parents as equals. Authority has never been impressed upon them, so they have no sense of authority or what it means, When a parent tells a child to do something, the response the child has learned is, "Let's discuss it." When a parent insists, the child is bewildered because he is not accustomed to that kind of treatment. The reaction is usually unpleasant. From then on it becomes impossible for the parents to exert any authority over the child without getting a broadside of abuse, or constant objections to every directive. This is quite normal for the child because ever since he was young, he was allowed to discuss everything and talk it over. As a teen-ager, it becomes a different ball game. He is no longer a kid, and he is no longer cute, and his problems and requests are no longer simple. When a parent has no argument against a child's position other than the parent's experience, the child can't understand. To try to impose authority at that late date is extremely difficult. Parents then, only too frequently, become violent and abusive, out of sheer frustration. This kind of behavior is foreign to the child, so he develops the attitude that the parents hate him, and the whole family relationship breaks down, frequently ending with the child leaving home.

Another problem that children have, who are on too friendly terms with their parents, is an inability to look up to other adults as different from themselves. They treat everyone the same, and are offended and indignant when adults treat them as children. Authority has little or no meaning because it was never a part of their family life.

Respect for another because of his position is difficult to understand because, in the child's mind, he's no different than anybody else. The child who has not been brought up to be sensitive to the subtle and complex system of titles and positions, and the seriousness with which people protect their hard-won titles, finds it almost too much to comprehend. Treating people as they expect to be treated is a whole new learning experience that often ends in strained relations and tense situations at work and in school.

Respect is a quality that has been noticeably absent in society, probably for a number of reasons other than what I have just mentioned, even though it is a necessity for the smooth conduct of our everyday affairs. Respect for others is really the mark of a highly refined person who has developed an appreciation for the gifts and the accomplishments of others. It is very much tied in with a person's attitude towards himself, and should be a quality parents would want to develop in their children.

I think, as parents read or tell stories about the life of Jesus to their children, they should point out the kindliness and courtesy of Jesus towards others. Even though shrewd, he was refined and polished in his handling of people, even difficult people. It is such a nice trait and so highly developed in Jesus, that children will easily find it attractive. Pointing it out to them is something that should be done frequently if it is to be effective. Also they should be taught how to imitate this characteristic of Jesus' life. For example, a child may be inclined to be bossy or over-bearing with children who are younger. It should be pointed out that the child is that way (usually they are not aware of the way they are acting), and taught to be more congenial and courteous. It is also good for parents to point out the good qualities and talents that other people have, so the children can learn to see the good in others and respect them for it. It shouldn't be done in a way, however, that will give a child a feeling of inferiority and make him downgrade himself. He can still be made aware of his own good qualities.

One of the things that disturbs many parents is the lack of respect children have for their age and experience. That is again something that children have to be taught constantly and from their early years. Children don't know what experience is; they haven't lived yet. So, how could they set a value on it? But, if parents shared some of their own experiences with their children, not in a bragging way, but in a way that children can get to know their parents and what their lives were like when they were growing up, the children would have a much better image of their parents, and they would feel much more confident in trusting their judgment. It is unfortunate, but so often true, children know nothing about their parents, except what they see around the house, and that usually is not very inspiring, nor does it lead a child to respect parents. But, if a mother was to tell a child what "daddy" was like when he was young, and help develop the child's image of his father, it would enhance the child's attitude towards his father. And the father should do the same for the child's mother. Children love to learn about their parents. They love their parents and want to know as much as they can about them.

If children have a good image of their parents and a deep respect for them, that respect shows in the way they treat other people. If children respect their parents, usually they respect others. If children have difficulty respecting parents, they frequently have problems with others, particularly those in positions of authority.

Respect is such a basic virtue that it usually affects various aspects of a child's behavior, and for this reason, parents should be willing to make the effort to develop in their children, attitudes that will engender respect. The parents' own behavior and example is of utmost importance in helping children grow in respect for parents, as well as for others.

THE CHURCH

The church plays a major role in the life of a Christian, and for that reason, it is essential and critical that a child be taught to have good feelings about the church. It is also important that the child have a precise idea of just what the church is, and what it was in the church that Jesus gave us as the great treasure, the pearl of great price, to which we should attach supreme value.

The child's first contact with the church is the physical building. That is the church for a child. When the child is listening to family discussions and hears people talking about the church, even though he doesn't know what they are talking about, he pictures the building and everything associated with it. The priest becomes part of that image, and becomes associated with all the feelings, good and bad, that parents' discussions breed in the child.

The church occupies such an all-encompassing role in our lives, that it is important that parents try to develop feelings in the child which he can feel comfortable with, and not have to go through life struggling with bitter, conflicting feelings about the church. The church, to a great extent, is an extension of the family, and of the parents' authority in children's lives. Children, therefore, naturally want to feel good about the church. When they hear parents criticizing it, they become confused and upset and insecure.

First of all, parents should make the children realize that the building is not the church, nor is the priest or minister the church. The church is the whole family of Christian people. In that family, some are priests or ministers who offer sacrifice to God and pray for the people, and reconcile people to God when they stray; others teach, others care for the sick, still others pray for the people and give help and support. All Christians are a part of the church. The idea that the hierarchy is the church is not healthy, and should not even be taught to the children. It is important that parents develop a true image of what the church is, so the children will have a clear idea to carry with them into adulthood. It will help them to avoid all kinds of problems later on.

Next, the children should be taught that the church is the embodiment of all the vast gifts that Jesus gave us, and that it is the function of the church to preserve and pass on to all generations these treasures of the spirit, the teachings of Jesus and the sharing of his divine life. The children should be taught to have a deep veneration for the church because of its close identification with Jesus, and because it enshrines the living presence of God in our lives. They should also be taught to respect what the priests or ministers teach and, particularly, what the successor of Peter teaches. The sacraments should be taught as the channels of God's life into our souls and essential to a healthy friendship with Jesus.

The Mass and the Eucharist should be taught as an intimate encounter with Jesus, and since religious services can become boring, the children should be taught to look beyond the sights and sounds in the sanctuary and realize they are in the presence of Christ and, through the eyes of faith, learn to see Jesus present there and communicate with him in the quiet of their souls.

This may all seem to be very idealistic, but I think it is only right that children should be given a chance to see what is beautiful, and to be able to enjoy feeling good about their church. As they grow older, they will hear people tearing the church apart and talking about this priest or that minister. They will need a really solid foundation if their faith is going to withstand the constant attacks on the church.

And although they may be taught when they are young that they should respect what the priest or minister says, and particularly what the successor of Peter says, that does not mean that, as they get older, they can't respectfully disagree, and be free to develop their own views, and form their own consciences, after having seriously tried to understand the thought and opinions of the clergy. Accepting what the church solemnly declares to be the teaching of Jesus is also an integral part of our faith. But there is a vast freedom of spirit to develop our own thinking, and even to disagree with matters that are only strongly held theological opinions, and personal convictions of even the highest authorities. But, for the sake of honesty and personal integrity, sincere Christians should make every effort to understand the church's position, and not just develop opinions contrary to the church's position based on superficial arguments.

Children can derive immense joy and comfort, as well as security, from association with their church and it is cruel to deprive them of that experience while they are still too young to understand the harsh realities of a critical and materialistic world.

TOLERANCE

Intolerance is the stunted vision of an undeveloped mind. A healthy and mature Christian should have an expanded awareness of the immense diversity throughout creation, and the unlimited variety of human viewpoints. The mind of a Christian should approach the mind of Christ, and the feelings and understandings of a Christian should be inspired by God's own awareness of the diversity of human experiences, and the variety of conclusions that can be drawn from those experiences. The more a person allows himself to grow, the more aware he becomes of the validity of others' experiences, and the more he respects their understanding of things. That is the basis for a tolerant mind. It is not necessarily similar to a broadly liberal mind that tolerates contradictions or justifies immoral behavior on the grounds of differing religious views. But, a tolerant person is realistic enough to recognize the fact of the wide diversity of human experiences, and still confident enough of its own vision to hold fast to strong convictions.

Looked at in this way, tolerance comes from breadth of vision and strength of character, rather than moral indifference. This way of thinking should be woven into a Christian's development from childhood. But, since the difference between indifference and respect is so fine, parents must really be careful in how they develop this mind in their children. It is not easy to teach a child to do his own thinking and to have strong convictions, and at the same time, respect the convictions of others who think differently from him. And yet, it must be done if the child is to develop a wholesome Christian spirit.

A child who grows up ignorant of his own faith cannot really be tolerant, because his own faith is uninformed. So, a child must first be taught to understand his own beliefs and to appreciate their beauty, and then be made to realize that others may believe differently, and feel just as strongly about their beliefs, and they should be respected even though we don't share their views. A child does not have to be taught that one is as good as another; in fact, that is ridiculous as well as unreasonable. A child has to be able to feel that what he believes is right. It is stupid to teach a child something, and then tell him that it may not be true. A child's character can grow only on a solid foundation of strongly held convictions. So, you can easily see the necessity of developing a comprehensive understanding of the teachings of Jesus and helping the child to develop a strong attachment to those teachings, and then, as occasion presents itself, teach the child how to respect the beliefs of others without compromising his own, and at the same time, not be afraid to express the reasons for his own beliefs in a gentle and kind manner. That balance in a person is rare, but should be the characteristic of every refined Christian. As strongly as Jesus felt about his own vision of life, he was always gracious towards those who were unable to share or even understand his vision.

But, there is a difference between Jesus and an ordinary child. Jesus could with good reason have confidence in his vision, but the ordinary human cannot be that sure of his own convictions without becoming narrow-minded. It is important that parents help their children to be open to the thoughts of others, so they can listen to what others think, compare it to their own views, and evaluate what they have heard. This is the way children grow intellectually; it is the way they expand their own understanding, and as they grow older, develop a depth and a richness in their thinking which provides the basis for growth in true wisdom.

CAREER AND VOCATION

Almost every parent sees a spark of greatness in their child. But, it is only the wise parent who will let the child grow the way God has formed him. Parents too easily form their own ideas about what their child should become, and many start from the child's infancy, to steer him or her in that direction, with little regard for the abilities, and with practically no regard for the child's own interests.

Parents must be convinced that God has a stake in their child. God created him and has a definite role for their child in his own plan. He has given the child abilities and talents, and a personality fitted for that role, and if the parents are willing to help, will guide the child to find his place in his plan. This is a necessity for the child's future happiness.

A wise parent will make every effort to understand their child and help the child to grow. To force a child to develop an ability he has no talent for, is like putting a left foot shoe on the right foot. It doesn't fit, and it hurts. Eventually it does damage that could be irreparable. But to watch and analyze and understand a child, to note his real abilities and interests should be the starting point for the child's development. If he has ability in music, art or mechanics, electronics, medicine or whatever, and if he shows an interest, the parents should encourage the child to develop that interest, either by taking those subjects in school if they are offered, or by arranging for private lessons. And parents should not be disappointed if their child is not academically inclined. Most children aren't, and if educators were wise, they would establish the majority of schools for vocational or mechanical or technical courses, and a small number of schools for the much smaller number of students who are academically gifted. There would be a lot less teenage crime if children were appreciated and their talents recognized by the schools, and efforts were made to prepare them for life. Children who are academically talented are well prepared by rich programming in the schools, while the manually or technically gifted, who may be geniuses in their field, are hardly ever adequately developed. By the time he or she is eighteen, a technically or artistically or musically gifted student should be already well-prepared for life, not still searching for a place to develop those talents. This is the great failure and disgrace of our educational system: its failure to recognize and appreciate and develop the talent of this vast number of gifted students.

While parents may not be able to get the help they need for their child in the school, they should try to provide some kind of help to develop their child's talents, because the use of those talents is the natural release for frustration, and the God-given therapy for depression, boredom and a poor self-image. And parents need not feel that their child is inferior just because he or she may not be good academically, but may be a good wood carver or artist or musician, or whatever. I doubt that Puccini, or Michelangelo or Da Vinci would have done well academically in our schools today. Those kind of geniuses are rarely good in academics. It is just unfortunate that we have the unhealthy image of college as the only gateway to success in life.

You may wonder what this has to do with religion, but if you look upon your child's talents as the key to his life's work, and his place in God's plan, then it becomes very much a part of the child's relationship with God, and essential to his healthy growth. As a tomato seed will grow into a tomato plant; and you can count on a healthy rose bush to produce roses, and not daffodils, so every child must be taught to grow in his own special way, and not be forced to grow in someone else's pattern.

TRUST

In our culture trust is not a very popular virtue, but it is the basis for Jesus' whole spirituality. As Christians, parents should have a deep sense of the supernatural, and of the intimate role God plays in each of our lives. Jesus pointed out the birds of the air as an example of our heavenly Father caring for his creatures, and assured us that we are worth more than all the birds of the air, so we should trust our heavenly Father to care for us.

But, we are afraid to trust God. Either we have our own pet plans and are afraid to trust God because he might have other ideas for us, or we are not really convinced that he is real, or is all that involved in our life to really do anything for us. But, whatever the reason, we don't teach our children to trust God, and we expose them to all sorts of emotional and psychological problems as a result.

Life is so complicated today, that if a child is conditioned to go through life depending only on himself, or even on other human beings, he is going to find himself in situations that are beyond human control, and where there are no predictable solutions. We can easily come to the frightening realization that we are very much alone on this earth and when we are in the worst predicaments, there is really no human being who can help – not even family.

When a person finds himself in these circumstances, where does he turn? If there is no sense of God and no feeling that God cares, he can only turn to himself, and since he has been unable to solve his problems, the options can be frightening.

A Christian has to be convinced that God is very much a part of his life, and his life is, indeed, a partnership with God, and God is always very close by, to help. He supports our efforts; he arranges circumstances; he counsels, guides and consoles. "I will send you the Holy Spirit who will befriend you," Jesus said. We should take Jesus seriously and believe him.

A parent who does not teach his child to trust God, leaves the child defenseless and vulnerable, and devoid of all those supports which Jesus intended to be part of our heritage as his followers. As Christians, we are a special people and Jesus promised us an intimacy and an accessibility to his friendship which should alter our whole life. Only parents can make their children aware of the beauty of their friendship with God, and how important it is as they go through their lonely journey on this planet.

But, trust has to be taught at a very early age. It is hard to teach a grown-up to trust, when he has learned to be a rugged individualist, or has learned that trust is weakness. Children very naturally trust. They have to trust because they are so dependent. If the parents are conscientious and dependable, a child can preserve this trust, and it can be easily transferred to his relationship with God.

If a child is brought up with faith, and his friendship with Jesus becomes real, he can develop good feelings about God and can learn to share things with him. If a child is taught that he should never worry, but always try to do his best; to sensibly work out problems, and trust in God's help, he can develop a strong, healthy confidence in God's support which will not be just talk, but the basis for a calm, serene attitude towards events in life. I don't think one could overestimate the value of that kind of trust. It is the key to peace and the key to a psychologically healthy emotional life.

How a parent should go about instilling trust in a child is not very difficult. When the child is young, and is facing little problems, parents can tell the child, "Now, let's not panic. We have a little problem that we have to work out. Let's talk to Jesus about it." Then help the child to tell Jesus, while at the same time assuring the child that the problem will be worked out. If the parent can keep calm, that in itself will go a long way to teaching that trust in God is real, and not just a lot of talk. If a child sees his parents feeling secure with God, then it will be a lot easier for him to feel comfortable, placing his own problems in God's hands. This is a good example of where the general family attitude is most important in teaching a religious value to a child. A stranger can do little more than just talk about it and give examples from others' lives, but that consistent everyday atmosphere of trusting in God has to come from the family.

One day, my sister Frances had hidden her older sister's school books, thinking she would have to stay home from school and could play with her. She told no one where the books were. When the older sister went to school, which was across the street, the little sister stood by the window looking across the street for the longest time, wondering what she should do. She decided to get the books and bring them to school. But she had a big problem. She was afraid of dogs, and there were two big dogs lying on the front steps of the school. She finally said to her mother: "I know Jesus won't let those dogs bother me. I'm going to bring Bernadette's books over to school." So she got the books and walked bravely right between the two dogs, who lifted up their heads, looked at her, looked at each other and went right back to sleep. Trusting in God gave her a lot of courage and strength, which she would not have had otherwise.

FORGIVENESS

It was only recently that the full force of Jesus' teaching on forgiveness struck me. Peter is the one who brings the issue up to Jesus when he asks Jesus how often he expects one to forgive. Jesus' answer, "Seventy times seven," bewildered Peter and everyone of Jesus' followers since. It is the one teaching of Jesus that most Christians just nicely ignore. We have qualified his answer in so many ways: "I can forgive but I can't forget," "I can forgive but, for my own benefit, I will have nothing to do with that person ever again," "Certainly God doesn't expect me to be a fool." With responses like these we glibly slide over this very serious injunction of Jesus. I have to admit, as hard as I tried all my life to understand what Jesus was driving at, it was only recently that I found the key to resolving the paradox and it seems to fit in with the way Jesus lived and thought.

Jesus did not teach the way religious leaders teach. We are concerned about dogma. He was concerned about sharing his life with us, his vision that would give meaning to our existence and bring peace to our lives on earth as we prepare for heaven. It is our lot as humans to be hurt and offended frequently during our lives. Jesus knew that and he also knew that if we continually allow ourselves to be hurt, it can ultimately destroy us. Peter was giving expression, to that experience when he asked Jesus,

"How often do you expect us to forgive, seven times?" thinking he was being generous. "Seventy times seven" was Jesus' shattering response. How could he be serious?

When Jesus taught something it was not to place an added burden on people; it was to simplify their lives or to heal. "The law was made for man and not man for the law," was Jesus' way of expressing it. So, when he taught his attitude on forgiveness, he was not decreeing an impossible command, but offering the solution to the most destructive sickness facing humanity. He was revealing the key to inner peace and to peace with others. What he is saying is not just forgive, but forgive totally.

Don't allow yourself to take offense when someone tries to hurt you. And that is a unique approach to insult. And when you examine the life of Jesus you can see he meant what he said, because he practiced it beautifully. Jesus seemed almost incapable of taking offense from the way people treated him. And they treated him shabbily and rudely. With all the miracles Jesus performed and all the good he did day after day, and all the cures he worked, there is only one incident recorded in the gospels where someone thanked him, and that man was a foreigner. You can't help but wonder. Yet, you never see him bitter or out of sorts or vindictive or hurt. He always treats people with such gentleness and understanding and the same even-temper. Even his enemies he treats this way. They would insult him one minute, then invite him to their house for dinner. Jesus would invariably accept, always looking for an occasion to heal, to shed light, to help them to understand.

I suppose it takes a big person, secure and confident of himself or herself as surely Jesus was, not to take offense when someone says or does something offensive. A person who is secure with himself or herself is not shaken by others' attitudes. It is the mark of a small person or a person with a poor self-image to be badly shaken by criticism or unkindness. A big person is more likely to rise above it or even laugh it off. One of the most beautiful traits in Jesus, one which dramatically exposes the divine qualities in his person, is his inability to take offense. He always seems to understand, which makes it possible for him to forgive and to overlook even the most shocking violations of his person. As soon as his enemies had stripped Jesus naked and driven spikes into his hands and feet and exposed him before the world, his first thought is one of forgiveness: "Father, forgive them; they don't know what they have done." Certainly Jesus practiced what he preached.

When I was a young boy (I guess I was about twelve at the time) on Good Friday one year, I was trying to be prayerful from noon until three out of respect for the sufferings of Jesus. I had found this old book in the cellar of an abandoned house. It was full of dust. I took it out on the sidewalk and browsed through it. It was full of stories. One of them touched me so profoundly I will never forget it. It was a true story about a family in France. They were very wealthy, and lived in a chateau. One of the butlers discovered the family's wealth in the vault under the house and decided to kill everyone in the family so he could possess the treasure. One night he methodically went about killing the parents and all the children. Only the youngest escaped.

Years later the murderer ended up on Devil's Island for entirely different crimes. The little boy also ended up there, but not as a criminal. After being orphaned for years he finally entered the seminary and became a priest. After ordination he was sent as a chaplain to Devil's Island.

One day, a convict came running into the chaplain's office. "Father, Father, come quickly. One of the men is dying in the field." The priest went and found the dying man lying in the dust. He knelt down by his side and rested his head in his lap and asked him if he would like to confess his sins. "No, Father, God will never forgive me for the evil I have done."

"God always forgives, my son," the priest said, trying to reassure him.

"But, what I have done is so evil," the man persisted.

"How evil?" the priest asked.

Then the man began to tell the story of the family that lived in the chateau, and how he had been their butler and one night murdered all the family so he could have their money, and how only the little boy escaped. The man finished by saying, "How could God forgive me for such an evil deed?"

The priest looked into the convict's eyes and with tears

in his own, said, "If I can forgive you, certainly God can forgive you. That was my family, and I am that little boy, and I forgive you from my heart." The two men wept together, and as the priest was saying the words of absolution, the man died in the priest's arms.

That story touched me so profoundly that it made me realize how beautiful was Jesus' concept of forgiveness, and how completely it can transform our lives.

It is important for parents to instill this sense of Christ-like forgiveness in their children's hearts when they are small, so they can start developing the habit of forgiving. Little Pete I mentioned before shocked me one night. It was a pleasant shock. His father had just given him an unmerciful bawling out. He was sent to his room. A short time later it was time for bed. Pete came downstairs and went over to his father, hugged him, kissed him, said "I love you, Dad. Good night." Then Peter went upstairs to bed. It was beautiful. I saw that same trait on other occasions. I was shopping at a computer store one day with him, and one of the salesmen was rude. I told Pete, "Let's go to another salesman. I don't want him to get the commission." Pete's response was, "Father, don't be like that. You're too big for that. The guy probably had a bad day." He taught me a lesson. That kind of mentality is beautiful to see. It is touching. And it is capable of transforming our whole society. So many of the stories in the news have to do with hatred and hurt and vindictiveness and pettiness that comes from hurt feelings. Even on the international scene, relations center so much around personal and national pride and sick competition, and the bruised egos that flow from all that kind of thing. Taking Jesus' message about forgiveness seriously seems to be the best antidote for much of the sickness that infects the world today. True forgiveness means not nursing wounds, and continually reaching out to reestablish relationships.

HEAVEN

Children spend most of their young lives in an imaginary world. It's very real to them. This is why it is so easy to teach children things of faith. Faith is not tangible; it has an aura of the make-believe, and because children feel so comfortable in that world, they readily accept stories about God and even miracles which they find fascinating. If faith is an important part of their young lives, what they are taught is incorporated into their normal thinking process and becomes a part of their real life and an important part of their value system, which, in turn, becomes part of their decision-making process.

Heaven is one of the teachings of Jesus, which children find most appealing. Because it fascinates them, parents should make serious efforts to teach them properly about heaven and not tell them things about heaven which will seem ridiculous later on.

Everybody has their own ideas about what heaven should be like. Little children like to think of it in terms of picnics and parties, and ice cream and candy, and all sorts of things pleasing to the taste. Teen-agers can't imagine heaven being very much fun unless sex is a big part of it. Older people become more curious as to what heaven could be like, because they realize that all their fantasies of the past about heaven were not too realistic.

While Jesus told us about the existence of heaven, it is interesting that he told us little else. St. Paul had a vision of heaven on at least two occasions and was lifted up to the third heaven on one of those occasions, and to the seventh heaven on the other occasion, but didn't tell us much more about his experience. St. John had a vision of heaven which he tried to describe in the book of Revelation. He described it as a kingdom of light; a place peopled by all sorts of fanciful creatures and filled with a radiance that emanates from the splendor of God's majesty. He talks about the music and the joy, and the happiness that fills this place where God lives. He talks symbolically of the friendships, and the companionship of all these beautiful beings; and the ecstasy that fills the soul when it sees God face to face. But all this is done with such confusing symbolism that one gets bewildered when he tries to put the images all together.

When parents talk to children about heaven, they shouldn't use the book of Revelation. It will only confuse them. They should talk to them very simply, but try to be honest and truthful and not make up stories that the children will have to reject later on.

One of the first questions children have about heaven is, "Where is it?" And you can tell them quite honestly, "It is all around us. Heaven is where God is and God is everywhere. Heaven is, therefore, everywhere, separated from us by just a thin veil, but all around us. It is a real world, but a world that exists in another dimension. If we had the power, we could pass through the veil that separates us from that dimension, and someday we will. It is like the story of Alice in Wonderland. When she passed through the strange entrance, she found herself in Wonderland. But even though we know Wonderland doesn't exist, heaven does exist, and one day, if we are good, we will be there.

When the children ask what heaven is like, it is good to describe it in terms they can understand. It is a real place, but unlike anything we will ever see on earth. You can take a child's experiences, like a trip to the ocean, or to Niagara Falls, or to any spectacular sight that impressed him, and recall how thrilled he was at the time. Then tell him that that is nothing compared to heaven. Ask him to recall the last time he came running to tell you how beautiful the sunset was, and how thrilled he was at seeing it. Then tell him that that is nothing compared to the beauty of heaven. Remind him of all the times he is happy and filled with joy over things that happen, and tell him that that is nothing compared to the joy and happiness he will have when he goes to heaven and sees God. You can also use examples of beautiful flowers and gardens and beautiful music; beautiful people and other things that appeal to him, to remind him of heaven. While the individual examples alone may not be too exciting, the accumulative effect of all the memories will be impressive, and should leave a striking impression on the child's imagination.

HELL

Although people don't like to believe that there is any place so horrible as hell, the idea of hell is not something the church invented. Jesus himself told us of the existence of this place created for the devil and his angels, and although Jesus never said any human beings have gone there, we have to believe the place exists. The images Jesus used to describe the place may be nothing more than symbols calculated to instill fear and dread of the place, but that there is a logical place where totally selfish persons go, people who have never learned to love anyone but themselves, that kind of place has to exist. Heaven and hell should be presented to the children as logical. It can be done in this fashion. Heaven is where God lives. There are some people on earth who try to do what is right, and live their lives for God and help others who need them. Their whole lives on earth are God-centered and filled with caring for others. When these persons die, they don't radically change from what they have been all their lives. Their orientation and attitudes are still God-centered, so their existence after death will be a logical continuation of their life on earth, but filled with all the joy and happiness of living in the presence of God.

On the other hand, there are some people who live their lives almost totally for themselves and for what they can get out of life. God, or the things of God, has little meaning for them, and people have value only if they can be used. The thought of helping others or of doing good for others is foreign to their interests. Persons like that are almost totally self-centered. Death will not change them. At the moment of death, they take with them the same attitudes and orientation they had the moment before they died. They are still self-centered and God has no meaning for them. They have lived their lives for themselves and their whole orientation after death will logically center around themselves. Since God was not, by their own choice, a part of their life on earth, it is only logical that after death he will not be a part of their life. They have freely cut God out of their life, so their existence in eternity will be an existence shared with others who have chosen to live without God and who cared little for others. What that place will be like is hard to picture, but it will be necessarily peopled by others who are almost totally self-centered. And that can really be a hell!

Whether hell is eternal is better to leave in God's hands. Jesus did say that it is forever, but Jesus so frequently spoke figuratively and symbolically to create a dramatic effect that it is difficult to know just how literally he intended himself to be taken when he spoke of hell. Also, whether their is any changing of attitudes because of a new understanding after death, there is no way we can know. Theologians and the teaching church can only go on the expressed thoughts of Jesus. Anything more is speculation. But God himself is not tied down to what he expressed, because he has not revealed all the qualifications and exceptions. So, there is always room to keep an open mind towards many things that may seem opposed to God's nature. Concerning the ideas expressed by Jesus, however, I am sure he intended us to take him seriously, so it is much wiser to act as if there is a hell than take chances on the speculation there is no such place. The surprise could be too great a shock!

DEATH

For a Christian death is not evil. God certainly should not be considered cruel or mean when he takes a person to heaven. But, because we become attached to our present existence on earth, death arouses horrible feelings in us. Because of the mystery and emotions surrounding death, parents should try to discuss this topic with children when they are old enough to understand.

Usually, the occasion of a death in the family presents the opportunity to discuss death, and to instill in a child a Christian attitude towards death. For a child to even begin to understand that death is not the end of everything, parents have to try to help the child to understand how God made us. All a child can see is the body. When a corpse is buried, all he can know is that it stays there and decomposes. To tell him about the person going to heaven confuses him.

I am still surprised at the number of Christians who have no idea of what the soul is, and yet, to understand the meaning of death, one has to have a clear understanding of the spiritual part of our nature. So, parents should try to explain that a human being is composed of a body and a soul. The soul is a spirit, like an angel. It is not some invisible being that has the shape of a man. We don't know what the soul looks like, except that it is much more beautiful than the body. Our thoughts and our love, and all that makes us what we are, comes from our soul. The soul, in some way, resembles God. When our body is first formed, God creates a special soul and unites it to our body. The body then becomes the instrument through which the soul works, like a violin which a musician uses to produce beautiful music. The genius lies in the soul. The body is the instrument used by the soul.

When a person dies, God calls the soul home. The body is left behind, like a baby bird leaving a shell. The soul is free for the first time, and lives the way angels live. When the soul was in the body, it was limited. It could only learn through the body's senses, which are like five little peep-holes to the outside world. When the soul is freed from the body, its ability to know and love and understand is unlimited. No longer tied down to the body, it can be anywhere it wants in a mere moment of time.

If the person was good and tried to please God on earth, then the soul will go to heaven. And where is heaven? Heaven is where God is, and God is everywhere, so heaven is all around us, just separated by a thin veil of time. Persons who die are so close, that we could reach out and touch them if we could reach into that other dimension where heaven is. So, our family members and friends, whom God has taken, are still alive and still close to us; so close they can hear us when we talk to them, and can help us when we need them, because they are still human and still care for us.

What happens to those persons who were not good? We don't know. Only God understands why they were not good, and God, in his mercy, is forgiving. But we still don't know whether anyone is so evil as to end up in hell. Jesus didn't even say that Judas ended in hell. All he said was, "It were better for him if he were never born." And that really doesn't tell us too much. So, we have to leave evil people to God. Only he knows.

It is also good to explain about babies who die. So often we look upon the death of a baby as a terrible evil. But, if God chooses to take a child to heaven, and allow it to live in heaven, and enjoy all the happiness of heaven without having to go through the problems and suffering of life on earth, that is a great privilege. God is not being evil or cruel or punishing anyone.

We were always taught that, if a baby dies without baptism, it goes to limbo. But we really don't know. Limbo is only an invention of the theologians. Jesus did not teach us about limbo. And Jesus never said unbaptized babies go to limbo. All Jesus said was, "Unless you are reborn of water and the Holy Spirit, you cannot have eternal life." He was not talking to babies. He was talking to grown-ups, who had done many wrong things in their lives, and needed to make the commitment of their lives to God if they expected God to save them. What God does with little babies, we just don't know. Certainly, God is not evil, and if we can be concerned for them, God, who is much more caring and merciful than we are, is more concerned than we are, and will certainly take care of them. So, there should be no fear or worry. All the good people who died before Jesus came, were taken to heaven, and they were not baptized. So, God is not limited in the way he deals with us. We may, as human beings, see everything as cut and dry, but God is not restricted by our understanding of how he should work. We have to trust in his love and kindness.

If a child wonders what happens to people who do not believe in God or in Jesus, we should tell them the same thing. We just don't know. God always rewards those who are sincere and care for others, and in their sincerity God sees them reaching out for him. He will certainly not push them away. If they are good, we can be sure God takes them to live with him.

FAITH

A very important idea for children to properly understand is faith. I don't mean that they should be taught as infants. In fact, some of the ideas we have been discussing may be too difficult for some little children to grasp. It is for the parents to judge when their child will be able to understand some things. While children can easily live in the world of faith, it is another thing for them to be able to understand what faith is. But, when they are mature enough to understand, it should be explained to them.

What is faith? First of all, it is not something unreasonable. We all have faith in someone. Little children believe everything their parents tell them, because they trust their parents to tell the truth. Religious faith is based on our confidence in Jesus. He proved he was the Son of God, and convinced us we should believe what he tells us is true. Since Jesus came from another world, heaven, we believe what he tells us about heaven, because we are convinced he is honest and truthful. There are also many ways that God has of looking at things, and many values that God has, that we can't understand. But because Jesus told us about these things, we accept them as true, even though we can't understand the reasons behind them. Faith in Jesus is no more unreasonable than a child's faith in his parents. If a being were to come from outer space and impressed us as being honest, when he told us about his experiences, we would have no choice but to believe him, especially if he looked and acted differently from anything we had ever seen. Jesus' behavior convinced the good people who listened to him that he had come from God. That was why they were willing to believe him. And that is why we have faith in Jesus' teachings.

Jesus also gave us the Church to teach us. We believe what the successor of Peter and the bishops teach, but not with the same kind of faith we place in Jesus. Very rarely are we obliged to believe on faith what the Church teaches. Many things the church teaches for our guidance, but not as a matter of faith. When the church does this, we respectfully listen and try to understand. If our own experiences convince us of the opposite, we may disagree. If the successor of Peter declares that what he is saying is what Jesus taught and that we must believe this as a Christian, then we accept what he says, because Jesus promised that he would be with the Church, and the successor of St. Peter, to guide and protect their teaching from error. Since Jesus told us this, we believe. But, it is very rare that the Holy Father speaks this way and declares something to be a matter of faith. It happens only once or twice in one or two hundred years; sometimes even less.

Faith should be taught to the children as something beautiful, not as something that restricts thinking or limits freedom. Faith gives us the vision of things we cannot see with our human eyes. It gives richness and depth to our understanding of life. It adds color and dimension to our lives, and makes the simplest things in life spring into our awareness with new meaning, and a feeling of joy and personal satisfaction. It helps us to understand things that perplexed the human mind from the beginning of time. It is a rich treasure, and the children should be taught to view it, not as a restriction on their freedom to think, but as an expansion of their vision into an unexplored world; a world they can know nothing about otherwise.

FAITH AND SCIENCE

We live in a highly technological culture. Our children's minds are saturated with science from the first moment they are allowed to watch television. In matters scientific, everything is predictable. It can be measured and accurately calculated. There is nothing accepted unless it is first proved. That kind of a mentality is just the opposite of the faith mentality, and if parents are not sensitive to the problems involved, and do not prepare their children beforehand, they run the risk of exposing their children to a gradual erosion of faith, and ultimately to a loss of faith. This happens frequently when students are deeply engrossed in science and are trained to prove everything from tangible evidence. When they realize that faith cannot be proved by measurable evidence, and is based upon the word of another, even though that person is Jesus, they find it very difficult to go counter to their well-trained thought processes, and accept something on faith, much less a whole way of life that is based on premises which demand faith.

It is vitally important that parents come to grips with this problem early in the childrens' life, because, if the reconciliation of faith and science does not become woven into the thinking of a child, he will find it next to impossible to make the adjustment later on. I was once attending a science convention, while I was still teaching science. One of the scientists at the convention sat next to me during the sessions, and we became friends. He had his doctorate in chemistry and taught at a college in Philadelphia with a high percentage of orthodox Jewish students. He himself was Jewish and was quite disturbed with the loss of faith among the science students. He asked me if I had any problem reconciling science with faith. I told him I had come to grips with the question a long time ago, and decided that there could be no inherent contradiction between the two, since God is the author of both. God cannot contradict in his revelation, what he has placed in nature. If science comes up with information that differs with something found in scripture, then you must use that information to shed light on the proper understanding of that part of scripture. Since scripture was written by human authors, they expressed what God communicated to them in terms of their own experience, education and understanding. God did not just use them as a pen, merely to write down what he directed. There is no evidence of that. God gave them insights and understanding of events which they had to interpret for the people in their own language, and through their own experiences, which were limited. These limitations imposed limitations on the clarity of God's message. Science can make valuable contributions to the understanding of the word of God, and we should never be afraid of it. I have never felt that my faith was threatened by science. I have always thought that science and revelation are two extremely valuable sources that complement each other, giving us deeper understanding of God and his creation from two different vantage points.

My friend was quite pleased with the simplicity of my solution to the question, and asked if I would be willing to come and lecture at the college where he taught. I told him I would be delighted.

But, there is another aspect of faith which has to be reconciled with the scientific method, and that is the acceptance of truths that are supernatural, or of a reality outside our tangible universe, like the existence of heaven or the nature of God. Jesus told us many things about God, the world beyond nature, and ourselves, which cannot be presently verified by science, and may never be. What scientists have to realize is that man's natural process of learning is not limited to the scientific method. All of us, even scientists, amass vast amounts of information through sources other than the scientific method. Every time a scientist picks up a book to read, he is laying aside his scientific method and placing his faith in the author of the book. We can't function without faith, which means placing confidence in persons who have deserved our trust. Jesus gave overwhelming evidence that he deserves our confidence in what he has told us. That is the very reasonable basis for our faith in him. A balanced person will, throughout his whole life, use various methods to arrive at the truth, sometimes faith, sometimes intuition, sometimes hard, cold facts. But each method useful in its own way and for its own purpose.

When a scientist uses his scientific reputation to convince students that there is no God, he has passed beyond the competence of science and wanders into the world of philosophy or faith. Science cannot prove one way or the other whether there is a God, because science only deals with the mathematical and the measurable, and God is beyond the reach of those limited tools. Science may wonder at, and dissect the very obvious and already existent world that lies before it, but it is helpless in trying to understand where it came from. An honest scientist will admit the inability of science to even approach that problem, because it deals with subjects beyond the range of the scientific method. Because these matters are beyond the focus of science, a scientist can, in good conscience, make the choice as to whether he wants to use a method of learning other than the scientific method to explore the world beyond the senses, without feeling that he is jeopardizing his integrity as a scientist. When he explores that world, he is doing it not as a scientist, but as an ordinary human being, searching out the meaning of his own existence which he can never learn from science. If he is to grow as a human being, he must do this.

I once watched on television a program which interviewed the famous scientist and missile pioneer, Wehrner von Braun. The interviewer asked him if, since he was such a great scientist, he found it difficult to believe in God. Von Braun was quite shocked by the question and answered, "Of course not. In fact, the more I learn about the universe, the more I stand in awe at the majesty of the God who made it." There was a man who was a great scientist and also a man of great faith.

That is the kind of mentality that we should try to develop in our children. In our sophisticated and highly technical age, we have to prepare our children to cope with these very unusual problems, which never existed in times past.

OTHER CHURCHES

It isn't long before the children realize that not everyone believes the same religion. I mentioned this briefly, earlier in the book when I discussed tolerance. But, it is important as the children grow older, to help them to develop a well-thought-through attitude towards other Christian religions. They can still be strong in their own beliefs and, at the same time, understand and appreciate how other Christian denominations came to exist. The original Protestant denominations broke from the Catholic Church because of abuses in the church, and an inability to be critical of church life and still remain happy within the church family. Tensions and conflicts made this almost impossible. It is interesting that many of the reformers never intended to break with the Catholic Church. Frequently, is was not they, but their followers who made the final break after the reformers themselves had died.

The Catholic Church has its roots firmly grounded in the original community that Jesus established, and even though life within the church was not always holy, and at times, even the hierarchy and the popes were not good men personally, the promise of Jesus to be with the church always, was still as valid during those times as it was during the times of the primitive Christian communities. Jesus never guaranteed holiness to leaders within the church; he promised to be with the church always, to protect the integrity of his message, and to assure the transmission of the divine life. Christians must always have to tolerate evil among their members, even among their leaders, as Jesus had to even with the apostles.

When the reformers broke with the church, they usually became strong witnesses to something that was seriously lacking in the life of the church. The church should have, in the past, and still can today, learn from that witness, and in its humility, correct itself and draw back those who have been alienated by its bad example and sometimes arrogance. This is an honest way of looking at the church; and it is not in the slightest way disloyal.

But, it is important to point out that not all those who broke with the church did so with noble reasons, as in the case of King Henry VIII. Also as time went on, groups broke away from the reformers and others broke from them, until now you have an unreasonable proliferation of Christian denominations, which scandalously fragments the message of Jesus and confuses not only Christians but non-believers as well, and jeopardizes the power and influence of the message of Jesus in a world that desperately needs to feel the presence of His goodness.

A child should be taught that, as Christians, we should not have a snobbish attitude toward other denominations. We can have the confidence of knowing that our roots go back to the earliest Christians, and we possess all that Jesus taught, but we should be humble in our realization that the church does not always manifest that by its actions. It is also important to point out that other Christians are baptized, and are just as much Christian as we are, and in spite of their religion not being the same as ours, they can be much holier Christians and more pleasing to Jesus in their own personal lives. Because of this we should not hesitate to worship with them if the occasion arises and invite them to worship with us. By our own understanding and tolerance we can each make our own personal contribution to healing wounds, and by our love draw many Christians closer to one another. This, I think, is a healthy way to view our relationship with other Christians. It is far different from the senseless mentality which says that "one religion is as good as another," and "we're all going to the same place."

JEWS

This, perhaps, is one of the most delicate and sensitive issues for parents who want to raise truly Christian children, and it must be faced honestly if we are to deal with it successfully.

I have seen, in otherwise good Christians, a suspicious and hostile feeling against Jewish people that shocked me. In some cases it was subtle; in others, it was obvious. I don't think it has anything to do with religion, but frequently stems from jealousy over the success of some Jewish acquaintances in business or finance, or the ability of Jewish groups to use political influence in a wise and shrewd manner, sometimes in issues that directly conflict with our own interests. Many times it stems from nothing deeper than a dislike for certain assertive individuals who happen to be Jews. But the important fact is that they make generalizations over the limited number of individuals they are acquainted with, and pass that hostility, undiluted and unrefined, to their children, who have to suffer the misery of growing with a bad feeling about people they have never met. It is sad; it is unfortunate; it is unchristian.

Children should be allowed to grow and develop their own feelings about people, and not be victims of their parents petty hatreds, hang-ups and suspicions. It complicates the children's emotional life in a way that is dangerous, and creates personal, emotional and psychological problems that will scar the whole rest of their lives. Children have the right to grow from their own experiences; free of their parents' emotional sicknesses.

I think parents should familiarize their children with the history of the Jewish people, and with the fact that they were chosen to receive from God the treasures of his revelation and to give Jesus to the world. For this we are grateful. Many of the Jews in the time of Jesus, and after his resurrection, became Christians, but not all of them. When we come across Jewish people today, we should not look upon them as guilty for not accepting Jesus because they know very little about him, and are not encouraged by Christians to learn more because, throughout the Christian era, Christians have persecuted Jewish people cruelly, and frequently, without reason. For much of their history, they have been unjustly deprived of their rights by nations which were predominantly Christian, and find it difficult to be trusting of Christian people.

That may not sit well with many Christian parents, but it is quite true, and forms a real basis for the difficult and tense relations that exist between Christians and Jews. The time has come for all of us to heal wounds. I am sure each of us has had bad experiences with some Jewish people. I know, I have. But for every Jewish person that I found abrasive or obnoxious, I have found an overwhelmingly greater number who were kind and gentle, and generous to a fault. I have found, if I am to be fair, perhaps an equal number of obnoxious people belonging to my own nationalities, but a more satisfying number of pleasant people. And I am sure that congenial Jewish people would react the same way to offensive Jewish persons as other people would. Human beings react pretty much the same under similar circumstances. So we really have very little justification for nursing petty prejudices which stigmatize a whole people for the difficult behavior of a minority.

However, there are some realities which must be squarely faced. The fact that the Jewish religion does not recognize the divinity of Jesus, presents problems for a Christian who is considering marriage to a Jewish person. For the sake of family harmony and personal peace, it is better if persons did not get involved in relationships this intimate, because of the serious danger of compromising one's conscience. For a Christian to deny the divinity of Jesus is just as horrendous as it is for a Jew to offer sacrifice to an idol and deny the existence of Yahweh. A person should never put himself in that kind of situation. But, people seldom pick whom they are going to fall in love with, so we find many Jewish-Christian relationships of this type. What should be the attitude toward such situations? Well, this is a matter that I have agonized over for years, and I think there is a solution which both religions can, in good conscience, feel comfortable with, or at least tolerate, if they can't feel comfortable with it.

Jesus, and the early Christians who were Jews, found no incompatibility in being Christians and remaining dedicated Jews. Had things worked out peacefully between these two groups, we would have seen Christianity as an acceptable branch of Judaism, with its Jewish members accepting Jesus as the Messiah, even though other Jews did not agree. There is a wide range of tolerance in Judaism, with the various interpretations of the law, and all are considered Jews. The concept of the Messiah is very much a part of the Jewish religion, and if some Jews feel a particular person is the Messiah, who can deny them that right? The fact that Jesus claimed to be one with God the Father, might present a problem. But even that is not insurmountable if those Jews who accept Jesus also accept his explanation that he was not another God but a different manifestation of the one God, a fuller revelation of the nature of this one God whom Jews adore. In this there is no contradiction with Judaism.

If that can be accepted by Jewish people, then the problem of marriage between members of our two religions is greatly eased because there is nothing in Judaism which a Christian can't freely accept, if he so chooses.

So if a Christian and a Jew marry, there is no compromise of conscience necessary. Both could teach the children about their own beliefs, and the whole family could attend, if they so chose, both religious services. The Christian could teach the children about Jesus, and the Jew could teach the Jewish faith, without fearing any serious theological conflicts. I am not saying this is something that should be encouraged, but it is better than demanding that one of the parties abandon his or her faith. That is intolerable. And where a couple are already deeply in love, and are on the verge of marrying, this solution should at least be considered.

NON-BELIEVERS

When parents have carefully and lovingly tried to nuuture a beautiful relationship between their children and God, it is a horrendous shock for a child when he meets a person who will very glibly say, "Oh! I don't believe in God. My mother said there's no such thing as a God."

Children should be prepared for such an incident. Just as parents can tell their children that not everyone believes the way their family does, they can also help the children to realize that some people do not believe in God. When a child asks, "Why?" parents can explain that some people have very difficult and sad experiences in their lives and get discouraged because they feel God doesn't help them. Sometimes they get angry with God. Also, many people who believe in God do not live good lives and seriously injure others. This may cause some persons to turn away from God. Then, there are some persons whose parents never taught them anything about God. And since it is almost impossible for a child to find out about God all by himself, the child may never learn anything about God. But, there are also some who are proud and vain about their own intelligence, and because of their pride, find it difficult to admit there is a God. None of the reasons seem to be too profound, but people feel they are justified in denying that God exists, so we should try to understand their feelings and not look down on them or ridicule them. Faith in God is a great gift, and we should thank God that he has given us the gift of faith, and all the beautiful things that enrich our lives.

I'll never forget an incident that occurred years ago when I was attending Columbia University. One of my science professors was alone on the elevator with me, and he said to me, "Father, I envy you Christians. Your faith seems to make you such happy people. I have never been able to believe in God, and I have tried so hard. My parents didn't talk much about religion or God, so he never meant anything to me. But, I wish I could believe." Faith enriches our lives, gives us a healthy image of ourselves, a sense of personal destiny, and an awareness of a beautiful life with God after death, so it can't help but fill us with a joy that should reflect in our daily life.

COMPASSION

The whole thrust of Jesus' teaching was aimed at making us more consciously concerned about the needs and sufferings of others. Indeed, in the only example Jesus gave of the Last Judgment, compassion was the sole criterion of God's decision as he reviewed each one's life on earth.

Some children seem to be born with a sense of compassion; but most children are so absorbed in their own interests that it doesn't occur to them to analyze the problems in others' lives. Becoming aware of others doesn't come easy because it entails a shift in the orientation of our concern, away from self and towards others. In most children, this will have to be done through the conscious efforts of a concerned parent. But it is well worth it. I think there is nothing more beautiful than a child showing compassion for another. Just think of all the people whose lives were touched by the Boys Town logo with the little crippled boy being carried on the shoulders of a fellow orphan boy, and someone asking, "Isn't he heavy?" and the response coming back, "He ain't heavy; he's my brother." It is children doing touching things like this that evidences future beauty of personality and greatness of soul, if parents encourage and inspire it.

Because compassion is so difficult to evoke in some children, parents may have to make an almost daily effort to draw out these tender feelings from their children. It can be done in a thousand ways. When you are with a child, and you come across a child with a physical or emotional problem, you could talk to your child about how difficult it must be for that little child to do many of the things that are so easy for us who are blessed with good health. Your child learns to look beneath the surface of things, when you talk this way, and begins to look in depth at people. After a while it becomes second nature for the child to view others, not on the surface of their lives, but for what they really are, and in the context of their own personal difficulties and problems.

Even children who have problems and handicaps themselves must be taught to have compassion and try to understand others. Frequently, they already have it, and it is so wonderful seeing the concern that many handicapped children show, particularly for each other. But, some children with problems can become resentful or self-pitying, and this can destroy their lives. These children have to be given special attention. Parents should draw them out of themselves and help them appreciate the gifts they do have, and teach them to compensate by developing those gifts to the fullest. They should be made to understand that God does not act haphazardly, and in giving them these problems, wanted to draw them specially close to himself, and accomplish something great in their lives. They can be taught, very effectively, and with great benefit to themselves, to have compassion for those who are gifted, but waste their gifts, or use them only for their own personal good. By their own courage and dedication, they can be a constant source of strength and inspiration to others.

Of all the virtues a Christian should practice, this virtue of compassion is, perhaps, the one that most closely approaches that quality in Jesus' life that reflects his divinity. That very touching incident when the pharisees brought the woman caught in the act of sin, and threw her at the feet of Jesus, demanding that he pass judgment on her, is a good example of Jesus' beautiful sense of compassion. He was so embarrassed for the woman that he turned away from the pharisees who were talking to him and ignored them. When they demanded a response, Jesus turned to them and said, "If you must condemn her, let him who is without sin among you cast the first stone." When they picked up stones, Jesus bent down and began to write in the dirt, seemingly, the secret sins of each one of the accusers. When they noticed, they dropped their stones and walked away, leaving the woman trembling at the feet of Jesus. Then, Jesus looked down at the woman and asked her, "Has no one condemned you, woman?" "No one, Lord." "Neither will I condemn you. Go and sin no more."

How beautiful! When you think how ready human beings are to condemn others for their sins, and demand that they be severely punished, the compassion of Jesus who alone was sinless, graphically accentuates the mean and petty hypocricy of human beings. This is seen in a sensational way whenever the issue of the death penalty is raised in the legislatures. One can't help but be reminded of the warning of Jesus, "Let him who is without sin among you cast the first stone." If one thing is needed in the world to bring the healing presence of Jesus into our midst, it is compassion for one another, and parents would do well to nurture this trait in their children.

COURAGE

To live the way Jesus showed us demands no little amount of discipline and determination. To follow Jesus for a lifetime in the face of hostile values, demands a courage that is not ordinary. Without that ability to withstand the pressures and continual obstacles to holiness, a Christian is left defenseless in his struggle for goodness.

And yet we come across Christians constantly who lack the courage to take a stand for what is right. We even see it, unfortunately, in religious leaders who are afraid to say what they really think about important issues, because it might affect their popularity or their promotions. How many people are unable to make decisions because they are afraid of being wrong or of upsetting others?

A wise Christian parent will recognize the value of teaching children to do their own thinking and make their own decisions. One can't emphasize enough the necessity of being trained to have courage to make decisions. So few people in positions of authority are able to make decisions that one wonders how our society and our churches even hold together, much less make progress.

One of the ingredients in the formation of courage is a healthy confidence in oneself. A parent would be hard pressed to develop courage in a child when the child is under a steady barrage of criticism. And there are many parents who feel that the way to discipline and teach children is by being critical of their behavior. Critical parents will only convince the child that there is something radically wrong with his way of doing things, and maybe even with his personality. It will be very difficult for a child who has become diffident about his ability to summon up enough courage to take a strong stand on an issue for fear he may be making a big mistake.

If parents want their children to be courageous, they have to modify their way of teaching their children, so they are not always criticizing them. They have to first build up confidence in the children as being intelligent and able to make decisions and bold personal choices.

I think much of what is behind parents' critical attitude towards their children's behavior is the supposition that their children are doing things wrong intentionally. Many things children do, they are not aware of. They are just not that introspective or self-conscious. Even grown-ups are not aware of the way they impress others. I think many parents could be much more kind in the treatment of their children. This doesn't mean that they can't be and shouldn't be firm, but that is different from being crude and critical and even abusive in the way they correct their children's faults.

Another ingredient in the developing of courage in a child is teaching a child how to make decisions. So many parents shield their children from difficulties, and would rather solve their children's problems themselves than see them frustrated or upset. It is much better, when a child has a problem, for a parent to teach the child to be patient and think about the problem, and come up with his own solutions, or to try different solutions, so he can see that there are a number of ways to approach problems. After a while, the child becomes expert in tackling problems and coming up with different solutions without his parents belittling him for his failures. He is just learning, and as he tries different things, he becomes more accomplished. Each time he succeeds, he becomes more confident.

With a strong feeling of his own ability to think for himself and make his own decisions, a person has a good support for taking an independent stand on an issue, and because of his confidence, is willing to face the opposition, knowing that what he has decided is right for him. If he has been trained to be patient and determined and willing to withstand hurt besides, he is well on his way to becoming a man of courage, and a leader of men.

LEARNING

Man is not just a computer that collects, stores, and retrieves data. Although he has that capability, and his mind is the most beautifully designed computer in existence, he is not just a learning machine. He is a person with a destiny, so there must be a well-reasoned philosophy behind his pursuit of knowledge. Before a person begins to learn, he must know who he is, where he is coming from, and where he wants to go. This philosophy becomes a built-in guidance system.

Parents must really try to understand and appreciate the differences in their children, so they can know how, and in what direction, to guide them. Schools are not much help in this because they are so hung up on the idea that college is the great savior of society that they paralyze personal ingenuity and growth. It is no accident that one of the most powerful creative phenomena today is the music that comes from young people; it has literally swept the world, and interestingly, for the most part, it is something they did not learn in school, but something they invent in their cellars and hangouts, with their buddies, many of whom are school drop-outs. Schools, with their rigidity and mass production of intellectual clones, molded and patterned after standardized testing, could not produce this unstructured and spontaneous form of creativity.

Wise parents will understand the limitations of the educational systems and not be afraid to recognize the individuality of their children, and help them grow the way God made them, to be themselves. In order to grow as a Christian, a person has to be himself. Each person has been made special as an individual, to fulfill a particular role, in an intimate partnership with God. To fulfill that role, each person has to be allowed to grow the way God intended, by not destroying or blurring his individuality, but by encouraging its development so he can become himself and be proud of who he is.

In order to foster this effectively, parents should have a well-thought-out and practical philosophy of learning that they can pass on to their children. It is a healthy thing for children to want to learn about nature and about people and animals and everything that fascinates them. All their energy, as young people, is directed toward satisfying their voracious appetite to learn. How to encourage and develop that deep-seated desire in a healthy way so that the children will be stimulated to learn more, and for the proper motives, should be a prime objective of parents. Too many children's pursuit of learning is poisoned by the fierce competition introduced to children once they enter school. Competition shifts the motive for learning from the healthy, natural desire to learn, to using knowledge as a tool to win rewards or to beat others. Learning then becomes warped because children will be stimulated to study just what they have to for a test or for some other narrowly defined objective. When that mentality takes hold of a child, it destroys his sense of wonder and the curiosity that once drove him to learn for the sheer love of learning.

The secret is for parents to provide a long range, consistent motivation that will stimulate their children's sense of wonder and curiosity, and the desire to satisfy that curiosity for years to come. That spells the difference between a really wise and learned person and a short distant achiever whose interest in learning only too often fizzles out once he graduates or gets his degree. That mentality is tragic in a doctor or a priest, or any person in whom people place their trust.

How should parents go about developing a good attitude towards learning in their children. First of all, they should help their children to understand themselves, and then develop realistic and attainable goals. The desire to learn is natural to a child. It's spontaneous; it's unselfconscious; it's free and it's unspoiled by self-seeking motives. To preserve the simplicity and purity of that desire to learn, and to fan the flame of that desire should be the objective.

I have noticed in some parents an impatience with children that makes me almost want to cry. I have seen children who have just discovered books and the wealth of fun to be found in them, but they can't read yet, so they ask their parents to read to them. I have watched the annoyance of parents who are too busy to be bothered to read stories to their children. And I have seen the spark of curiosity snuffed out before it ever had a chance to glow.

Another manifestation of children's desire to learn is the constant need to touch things, and to take them apart. Parents look upon it as a destructive tendency. And they punish them for being destructive. It is not destructive; it is the way they learn, and rather than yelling at a child or punishing him for touching something, as if he was doing evil, wouldn't it be much better for parents to have old clocks or old toys, or simple harmless machines available to the children, so they can freely take them apart and satisfy their curiosity. They would much rather do that than play with new toys which they are going to try to take apart anyway after they have them for a short time.

It may not seem very scientific, what a child does to things, but it is the very same thing a scientist does. He takes it apart and then analyzes every piece. Unfortunately, children rarely put things back together in good working order; but then, even scientists can't put back together the masterpieces that God has created, after they have finished dissecting and analyzing their infinitely complex simplicity.

When Peter was a little baby, I used to ask his parents if I could take him for a trip up the street. I wanted to try an experiment. He was, I think, a little less than a year old at the time. It was winter and the snow had just fallen. Carrying him in my arms, I let him touch everything: the snow, the bark on the trees, the ground, the metal light pole which I banged with my knuckles to make it gong, the dead leaves, the automobiles parked along the sidewalk and everything we looked at. As we touched something, I would say its name. I had no idea how much he understood, but I noticed how much he enjoyed touching things. Each week I did this when I came to visit. When the summer came, we looked at all the flowers. At first, he would grab them and pull them off the stems. Then I took my right hand, separated my index and second finger, and placed it under a flower, and we bent close to look at it. I would say, "Flower, pretty flower."

Even though there was no way I could tell just what he was absorbing, I knew he could see and hear, and had a memory. Not many months later, when he had just begun to talk, I intentionally took him on a walk along the exact same street. What a shock it was to me, as we approached each object, he pointed it out and called it by name. When we approached the light pole, he made a little fist and wanted to knock at the pole. When we touched the tree, he rubbed his fingers across the bark, like I showed him, and he said, "rough."

While the experiment may seem simple and maybe not too important, I felt it did two things that were important and which parents may not ordinarily appreciate. It opened an avenue of communication with a child at an age that parents may think too young. It also served to stimulate that baby's curiosity to learn, and experience many more things in nature than he might otherwise.

The finishing touch to the story occurred years later. The boy was, I think, about six years old. His family had planted some new flowers in their garden. When I came to visit one week, he brought me out to the garden to show me the flowers. Bending down, he separated his two fingers and placed them underneath a flower and commented, "Isn't that pretty?"

Since one of the chief sources of knowledge for a child is reading, children should have pleasant experiences with reading from their early years. If parents take the time to read stories to their children, it whets their appetite for more stories. If the reading of stories becomes normal activity for a child each night, eventually, the habit becomes so ingrained, that the child will automatically tend to read a book at night rather than watch television. It is such a rewarding surprise to see a child bringing books home from the library, and not being able to wait until he can get a chance to read them. If the habit of study is developed at an early age, it will help to keep alive the beautiful curiosity that should inspire a child.

Children's developing interests are another evidence of growth in learning. Sometimes, however, a child may show a liking for something the parents may not approve of, say, for mechanics, or painting. Some parents may be terrified their child may be showing symptoms he is not college material. The parents panic and immediately try to discourage the child's interest. That can be devastating. He may never get interested in anything else for years, and most certainly, not in pure academics, if he doesn't have the interest or capability. It is much better for parents to be realistic about their children and accept them for what they are, than try to make them into something they can never become, or even if they do become, do so most unhappily, with the risk of destroying their future. Knowledge and the development of talent must flow spontaneously from the natural curiosity and ability of the child himself. It cannot be programmed artificially by another who wants to relive his or her life vicariously in their child.

Taking time to notice the interests of children and being patient to encourage and develop those interests is the key to starting children on the rich and rewarding path of knowledge and self-development.

CREATION

When a child reaches the age of wonder and begins to ask questions about God and creation, parents may be confused as to what they should tell him. For example, a child may be listening intently while a mother explains that God created the world and everything in the universe. The mother looks at her child and feels proud at the child's absorption in her story-telling, not realizing that he is getting ready to ask the next question, which is a real "zinger." The child looks innocently up at his mother and says, "Mommy, I understand all that, but who made God?" The mother can't very well tell her child that no one has been able to satisfactorily answer that question. The child wants to know.

Of course, the best answer is to be honest and tell the child that we just don't know. The world is here, all around us, and it can't make itself, and since it's made so beautifully, it must have been carefully designed. It had to be made by someone very wise and full of love. That person we call God. But, we don't have any idea of how God exists. He's different from us and we have no way of understanding him, except from what he tells us.

The story about Adam and Eve is also important because it provides the background for understanding the meaning of redemption and the purpose of Jesus' coming. There have been so many ways of explaining the story of Adam and Eve, some good, some bad, but I think the best way to explain it, and a way which doesn't nave to be reinterpreted later on, is to tell the children that God made our first parents, whoever they were, (we really don't know their names), and placed them in a beautiful part of his creation. God wanted very much for Adam and Eve to love him, but did not want to force them to love him. He made them free and gave them all kinds of special gifts. They were free from sickness and ignorance. They were unusually intelligent and were at peace with themselves. And if they remained loyal to God, one day God would take them to heaven with himself, so they could be with him forever.

Besides all this, God shared with them his own life and allowed them to walk with him in the garden at evening time.

But Adam and Eve had a big choice to make. They had to decide whether they would love God and serve him, or whether they wanted to be independent and do as they pleased. They finally decided that they would prefer to be independent, and live the way they chose. Once they made that decision, they lost all the special gifts God had given them. They even lost God's friendship and the beautiful life he had shared with them; a life that they were supposed to pass on to their children. But, now that they had lost this gift, their children were born without God's friendship and his life, which is necessary if we are ever to see God.

God realized what a horrible mistake Adam and Eve had made, and that the whole human race would be affected by their selfishness, so he immediately promised one day to send someone who would bring the whole human family back to his friendship, and share with them his divine life. Later on, God was to send his son, Jesus, to offer his life for all of us, to show God's love for us, and to share with us his own divine life. By doing this, we would all have a chance to come back to God's friendship and live with him in heaven.

Explaining things in that way puts the whole Old Testament into proper perspective, and lays the foundation for understanding the necessity for Jesus' coming and for redemption.

Since children will be confronted with so many problems about creation later on, it is also good to talk about how God created. Whoever developed the story of creation in the bible did it very beautifully and artfully, but did not intend to describe precisely how God did it. When we study in school about the history of the earth, we learn that life was much different many hundreds of millions of years ago. At one time, there were huge dinosaurs and fern trees and practically none of the animals and plants we see today. Then those animals and plants disappeared and new ones took their place, so that now we have a vast variety of all kinds of things. Did God make each of these types of plants and animals himself, and did he initiate each of these great changes in nature directly, or did he place in the original matter he created the coded blueprint for change, so that all the wonders which he hid in creation would gradually unfold and appear in different stages of time?

There is no way of knowing just how God creates and brings about change in his creation. God could have done either. There is evidence for both, but many scientists today think that life forms evolved in the course of billions of years until they developed into the types of plants and animals we see today. That may well be the way God did it; it is certainly very much like the way God works in nature. Growth patterns and change are found everywhere in plants and animals, why should not that same process be at work in God's overall masterpiece of creation? As Christians, we can feel comfortable with either story, or whatever scientists may one day prove to be fact. But until then, we are free to pick our option and believe whichever theory appeals to us as the more reasonable. In the end it may be a combination of both theories that will most accurately point to the way in which God directs his creation. For those who believe in God there are many options open; for those who do not believe in God there is no explanation but chance for the yawning gaps in the evolutionary process.

JESUS – HIS BIRTH AND RESURRECTION

The beginning and the end of Jesus' life are filled with mystery. From a theological viewpoint, they are also the most important events of his life. Because of this, parents should attempt to be as precise as possible in passing on to their children an understanding of these events, so that later on they won't be jolted by the oft-occurring speculation about the life and resurrection of Jesus.

Although he wasn't called Jesus, the person of Jesus existed before he came to earth. He existed throughout eternity as the living Image of the eternal God, whom we refer to as the Father. This Image of God we call the Son of God because he came forth from the Father, and it is easier to think of him as the Son of God, because we can better understand this kind of expression.

When God decided his Son should come to earth, he prepared for him a human mother, whom we know as the Virgin Mary. At the appointed time, the Son of God entered the womb of the Virgin Mary, took from her his human body which was enlivened by a human soul specially created for him, and thus became the Son of God in the flesh, whom we call Jesus. So, you can see that this Jesus was a divine Person who had two natures: the divine nature as God's Son, with his divine mind and divine will, and a human nature as Mary's Son, with a human body and soul. It is important to remember that there were not two persons in Jesus, one divine and one human, but only a divine Person who had assumed a human nature.

When, after nine months, Mary gave birth to Jesus, in a way that miraculously preserved her virginity, she could really be called the Mother of God because her Son was a divine being. In calling her this, we realize that she did not create God, but since her Son was not a human person but divine, when she brought forth her Son, she gave birth to a divine Person.

When we look at that helpless baby lying in the manger at Christmas, we really view a great and unspeakable mystery. That baby's brain is the seat of the divine intelligence that designed the vast machinery of the universe and comprehends each detail of every individual creature's destiny. His human will enshrines the omnipotent power that controls the whole of creation. And we see him, stripped of power and majesty, shivering in the cold, smelly air of the stable, to set example for us and teach us the true values of life, values hidden beneath the attractive things that appeal to us most.

At the end of his inspiring life, he was arrested, judged misfit for life among us, and nailed to a cross, where he died. Since he had no earthly possessions, he was buried in another's tomb, but, three days later, while the trembling earth broke open the tomb, it was revealed that the body had already left. He had miraculously risen from the sealed tomb, like sunlight passing through a window, and later appeared on many occasions to his followers.

The evidence that Jesus had risen from the dead was overwhelming to the people of his day, and the force of that evidence has not diminished with the passing of time as he promised to make his presence felt by those who sincerely and humbly accept him.

These are the basic truths in the life of Jesus. I realize the full implications are beyond the grasp of children, but I put them here as a touchstone for parents to use when they are talking to their children about Jesus, so they can have a solid understanding, as the departure point, when they go off on their own to tell stories about Jesus.

Parents should frequently take the gospels and read short sections of them to the children, and try to explain the scene to them, being careful to draw out of the incidents an appealing description of the personality of Jesus, so the children can become attracted to him and begin to feel close to him. This kind of relationship can blossom into a beautiful friendship with Jesus which will color their whole understanding of religion and have a powerful effect on their lives.

HOLY COMMUNION

It was not for shallow, flimsy reasons that Jesus promised to give his flesh and blood as the food of our souls. He was ever conscious of the loneliness each of us experiences as we go through life. He knew we needed to sense his closeness, so he offered to become present to us, in a special and more intimate way than his ordinary presence throughout the universe. He offered us the privilege of drawing close to him in Communion whenever we felt the need, and know for certain that he is present in a special and intimate way for those few moments, to give us strength and consolation and encouragement.

This great gift of Jesus should be the cause of continuous joy for Christians. When we realize the implications of the intimacy of this contact with God, it should have a profound effect on our lives and be a living proof of the Resurrection.

It is hard to imagine Christian parents not deeply attached to Communion, not just for the benefit that they can gain for themselves, but because of the effect it can have on their children. Of all the things we believe as Christians, there is no belief more dependent on parents' example than the Eucharist. Strong faith of parents convinces children of the reality and seriousness of the presence of Jesus in Communion. A lack of interest on the part of parents, on the other hand, is the strongest evidence to the children that Jesus is not really present in Communion.

Because Communion is a meal, it should be a regular event in the life of the family, something that the family prepares for together, with a real spontaneous joy and enthusiasm. It should be a natural expression of the children's friendship with Jesus, and not just something kids do when they reach seven years of age, as if First Communion was totally unrelated to their ordinary life.

It has been the custom in the past and is still quite prevalent, to start preparing children for their First Communion when they are in the second grade. That is helpful only if there has been a continual preparation previous to that at home. As I mentioned earlier, a shocking number of children stop receiving Communion and going to church right after First

Communion, because it is just not a normal part of their family life.

If Communion is to be a meaningful experience for children, it has to be woven into the fabric of their friendship with Jesus. It cannot be just a goal they arrive at, when they are seven years old. Parents should have been developing a strong relationship with Jesus all along, so, when Communion time comes, the children are thrilled at the thought of Jesus coming into their souls. Their solid friendship with Jesus will encourage frequent Communion afterwards.

I write this from experience. When one of my sisters was little, she fell in love with Jesus. Sunday after Sunday, she would cry when the rest of the family went up to receive Communion. She would ask, "Why can't I receive Jesus, I love him so much?" But, the rule was you had to be seven years old. So, she had to wait for over two years before she could make her First Communion. But the day she finally received Communion, she was so rapt in ecstasy, that the family couldn't distract her to take her picture. Since then, Communion has always been an important part of her life.

I tried this same procedure with little Joey. When he stayed overnight at the rectory, he would come to Mass with me in the morning. Since he was only four and a half at the time, and not allowed to receive Communion, I would give him an unconsecrated wafer after Mass. One day, when he was five years old, he said to me, "Father, I don't want to receive the make-believe Jesus anymore. Why can't I receive the real Jesus? He's my best friend, and I love him so much."

That's the way it should be. Joey made his First Communion at five. Now, he's thirteen and still treasures the intimacy with Jesus in Communion.

If parents want to see faith blosssom in their children's lives, they must develop a sense of the reality of Jesus' presence in the family, fostered by a deep devotion to the Eucharist. There is, perhaps, nothing that can have so profound an effect on the life of a Christian than a mature and intimate relationship with Jesus in Holy Communion. "He who eats my flesh and drinks my blood lives in me and I in him," Jesus said. If Christians only realized the power of that promise!

THE BIBLE AND THE CHURCH

The Word of God is the indispensible nourishment for spiritual growth. A person can be holy, perhaps, and lead a good life without reading the scriptures, but if a person wants to develop depth to his spirituality, his inner life must be fed a steady diet of God's word. This is so because the Word of God contains a rich and comprehensive insight into the mind of God, and reflects a viewpoint that is uniquely divine. As a person reads the scriptures and adapts them to his own life, he gradually begins to think the way God thinks, and governs his life according to the pattern found in the scriptures. The wisdom and understanding of God begin to reflect in the life of the person, as he becomes more and more identified with God.

But, as important as the sacred scriptures are for the life of the individual Christian, as well as for the life of the church itself, it must be made very clear to children the precise role the scriptures play in the church. It is important and interesting that Jesus never told the apostles to write. He gave them the command to go out and teach all nations. St. Paul said that we learn faith from hearing. The Word of God was spread for decades before a single word was written down, and St. John says that what was written down was very little compared to all that Jesus said and did, thereby, testifying to the incompleteness of the written word.

What was important to Jesus was the establishment of the kingdom of God on earth as the vehicle of God's continued presence among men, and as the custodian of his teachings. This church was to be the depository of faith, and Jesus promised to be with her always, even till the end of time, and guaranteed her fidelity in the transmission of his revelation.

He promised also to send the Holy Spirit who would bring back to her mind all the things that Jesus taught, and gave her complete authority over his Word.

In doing this, it is not as if Jesus was setting up an authority independent of himself. It was his way of expressing his intention to be present with the people of God throughout history, to be with his people, his church, to assure them of protection and his never-failing guidance, so that what he taught in Galilee, originally, would be taught in its completeness to all people in future generations who would open their hearts to receive his message of salvation.

From the many and contradictory interpretations individuals place on the written word, it is obvious that the Holy Spirit does not deal directly with individuals in guaranteeing the integrity of Jesus' revelation, so it must be with those whom God calls to succeed the apostles that he gives his continued assurance of infallible guidance. Without going too far, we can understand the necessity of God working this way. If he had any concern whatever for the integrity of his revelation and the importance of that revelation being transmitted intact to all peoples of the future, he had to take this measure to protect his revelation.

It is to the church, then, that the Christian people should primarily look for guidance in matters of faith. The New Testament has value because it was written by the early church to whom Jesus gave authority to teach his Word, and the church can always be looked up to for authentic understanding of the mind of Jesus. I am not saying that church leaders themselves will be perfect reflections of Jesus' example, but because of Jesus' own promise to us, we can be sure that what the church teaches has the stamp of Christ's approval, and the seal of the Holy Spirit's promised guidance.

If Jesus meant what he said, that the Holy Spirit would be with the church to guide it; then, it must be assumed that, during the past nineteen hundred and some years, the Holy Spirit has been guiding the church, bringing back to her mind more and more of what Jesus taught. If this is true, then the teachings of the church today should reflect a growth and maturity in understanding of the mind of Christ that would be significantly more developed than what is expressed in the written word of the first century.

As a Christian looking for guidance I cannot take the scriptures separated from the teaching church and expect to find the complete message of Jesus. An accurate understanding of the relationship between the church and the scriptures is critical in developing a balanced understanding of how Jesus' revelation is transmitted from one generation to another throughout the whole of future time, and still preserved intact.

EPILOGUE

I have tried, in these pages, to discuss some approaches and attitudes, which, from experience, I have found to be essential in the early development of a Christian mentality. I realize that others may have thoughts and convictions which differ from my own and may be just as valid. I also realize that, what is written here, is far from complete. The ingredients which go into the development of Christian character are many and, also, complex. But it is my hope that, as simple and as incomplete as my approach has been, parents may find some help in the very confusing and difficult task of raising their children to be Christians after the heart of Jesus himself, and of molding their children to become the beautiful, free people that Jesus wants them to be.